LOW CHOLESTEROL
- COOKBOOK -

365 Days of Quick & Easy Low Sodium and Low Fat Recipes
to cut Cholesterol and Keep Your Heart Healthy

2022

★ ★ ★ ★ ★

Sarah Stone

TABLE OF CONTENT

What is Cholesterol?

Cholesterol is a fat present in the blood, most of which is produced directly by the body and a minor part is introduced through the diet. In physiological quantities, cholesterol is necessary for the correct functioning of the body, but it is necessary to measure it to monitor that the situation does not change because an excess can have negative consequences on the body.

Difference between LDL Cholesterol and HDL Cholesterol

When we talk about cholesterol, it is necessary to make a distinction because there are two main types of lipoproteins: on the one hand there are low-intensity lipoproteins, defined by the acronym LDL, and on the other hand, high-density lipoproteins, defined by the acronym HDL. The first ones identify the "bad" cholesterol because they transport the excess cholesterol from the liver to the arteries, while the second ones identify the "good" cholesterol because they implement the removal of cholesterol from the blood, protecting both the heart and the blood vessels.

For this reason, the cholesterol that is measured through blood tests can be summarized as a sum of LDL and HDL.

LDL Cholesterol

LDL is a vital lipoprotein responsible for transporting cholesterol in the blood through the body. However, most people have LDL levels that are too high, which are likely to accumulate within the walls of blood vessels where it is trapped and modified: this represents the beginning of the formation of a so-called "atherosclerotic plaque". These plaques can grow in any blood vessel in the body, including the heart, legs and brain. The more cholesterol trapped in the plaque, the more it increases. When it becomes large enough to partially block blood flow in heart vessels, it can cause symptoms such as "angina" (chest discomfort) during exercise. A completely blocked artery that supplies blood to the heart leads to a heart attack. It is the top cause of death in the Western world.

Very high levels of LDL cholesterol (> 190 mg/dl; > 5 nmol/l) Should prompt a second opinion, as familial hypercholesterolemia is possible. Lifestyle changes can reduce LDL cholesterol by about 10-15%. If this is not enough to achieve baseline values, medications like statins or PCSK9 inhibitors may be taken.

HDL Cholesterol

Usually called "good cholesterol", because high HDL levels were associated with a lower incidence of heart and vascular disease, this view has changed over the past few years. HDL values alone tell us nothing about the quality of HDL cholesterol. In addition, studies show that increasing HDL levels by taking medications did not reduce heart disease. Therefore, HDL levels should not be used to analyze risk, including so-called "ratios," according to which high HDL levels may offset high LDL levels.

Normal Cholesterol Levels

According to blood experts, total cholesterol levels should be managed below 200 mg per deciliter. LDL cholesterol should ideally not exceed 100 mg/dl, although levels below 160 mg/dl are normal. Finally, HDL cholesterol should equal or greater than 50 mg/dl1,2. Total cholesterol is considered "moderately high" when blood concentrations are between 200 and 239 mg/dl and "high" when they reach or exceed 240 mg/dl. On the other hand, LDL cholesterol concentration is considered "near-optimal" for values between 100 and 129 mg/dl, "moderately high" for values between 130 and 159 mg/dl, "high" if between 160 and 189 mg/dl, and "very high" if it reaches or exceeds 190 mg/dl. HDL cholesterol is considered "low" when blood concentrations fall below 40 mg/dl and "high" when equal to or higher than 60 mg/dl2.

Cholesterol levels for adults:

AMOUNT (mg/dL)	TOTAL	LDL	HDL	TRIGLYCERIDES
NORMAL	<200	<100	>60	<150
BORDERLINE	200-240	130-160	Women: 40-60 Men: 50-60	150-200
TOO HIGH	>240	**High:** 160-190 **Very High:** >190	Women: <40 Men: <50	**High:** 200-500 **Very High:** >500

Risk Factors for Developing High Cholesterol

Several conditions are associated with the development of high cholesterol. These include being overweight, obesity, an unhealthy diet, smoking - which in the long term damages blood vessels and accelerates the hardening process of the arteries - and lack of physical activity. Some metabolic diseases, such as diabetes, are often associated with hypercholesterolemia. On the other hand, some individuals are genetically predisposed to develop hypercholesterolemia, a condition known as "hereditary or familial hypercholesterolemia" and is associated with a series of genetic mutations.

The Foods to Be Preferred

The diet plays an essential influence in the control of plasma cholesterol levels: the correction of dietary style, in mild forms, can be the only therapy, but also in association with drug therapy, an adequate diet can enhance the effectiveness of cholesterol-lowering drugs and allow to reduce the dosage and any side effects.

Here, from the experts, the advice on foods to put on the table:

Vegetables, cereals and legumes are the friends of the heart. Therefore, setting up a dietary pattern is a good idea to consume these vegetable foods. In particular, it is good to eat legumes 2 to 4 times a week (which help to maintain adequate levels of cholesterol due to the presence of fiber and plant sterols) and 2-3 portions of vegetables and 2 of fruit per day (which reduce the calories in the usual diet and contribute with the vitamins and antioxidants they contain to reduce the overall cardiovascular risk).

The correct seasoning: cholesterolemia is influenced by the type of fats in the diet: saturated fats, of animal origin, cause an increase in LDL-cholesterol, while unsaturated fats, of vegetable origin, can lower it and help raise the good one. In particular, avoid butter and lard in favor of polyunsaturated or monounsaturated vegetable oils such as extra virgin olive oil and seeds (soybean, sunflower, corn, peanut). Even rice oil can be interesting for controlling cholesterol due to phytosterol gamma oryzanol.

Less fat: when talking about fats, it is necessary to pay attention to seasonings and limit the ones naturally present in foods. Sausages, cheese and eggs contain high quantities of fats, and if consumed in excess, they can negatively influence cholesterol levels. As for dairy products, it is better to favor skimmed or partially skimmed milk, yogurt with a low percentage of fats, and cheeses with fewer fats.

Fiber is a vital aid: vegetable fiber reduces the intestinal absorption of fats. One more reason to reserve a place of honor on the menu for legumes and vegetables, the latter possibly consumed raw in salads. Bread should be preferably whole because of its higher fiber content, as well as pasta and rice. Oats, barley and spelt are also suggested.

For the particular composition of its fat, bluefish can be consumed even by those who have cholesterol problems. On the contrary, consumption of at least 2-3 times a week, except for molluscs and crustaceans to be limited to one - is even recommended, with a preference for small-sized fish such as bluefish (e.g. sardines and mackerel), cooking it in the oven, baked in foil, steamed and avoiding frying as much as possible.

Meat can be part of the diet, with a preference for white meat, but it must come from a lean cut and without visible fat. Poultry, instead, must be skinless.

Fat-free cooking: prefer boiling, stewing, steaming, and traditional and microwave baking or grilling as cooking methods rather than frying or barbecuing.

Foods to Limit or Avoid

To keep cholesterol under control, experts suggest limiting:

- **Animal fats** such as butter, lard, lard, cream
- **Saturated vegetable oils:** palm and rapeseed
- **Offal** (liver, brain, kidneys), sausages with a high content of saturated fats. Sausages and preserved meats, in general, should be consumed as little as possible for cardiovascular prevention and the prevention of cancer. The guidelines suggest not to exceed 50 grams per week.
- **Whole or condensed milk**, whole yogurt, cheese with high saturated fat content
- **Alcoholic beverages** (especially in cases of hypercholesterolemia associated with hypertriglyceridemia)
- **Simple sugars** such as glucose, sucrose and industrial fructose

Lifestyle

Nutrition, however, is not always enough. It must be backed up and supplemented with a healthy way of living.

Experts recommend paying attention to:

- **Don't smoke**, as smoking lowers your 'good' cholesterol levels (as well as damaging your arteries).
- **Practice physical activity** that increases 'good' cholesterol at the expense of 'bad' cholesterol. The choice should always be made in the context of aerobic sports, such as cycling, aerobic gymnastics, dancing, swimming, soccer, basketball, volleyball, brisk walking.
- **Eliminate pounds** and especially excess waistline.
- **Check with your doctor for any co-existing conditions**, especially high blood pressure and diabetes mellitus.

Start by improving your diet

Nutrition is the place to start when it comes to keeping your cholesterol in check, but don't jump into DIY diets.

We've assembled some mouthwatering recipes to make it easy for you to start incorporating some of these changes. By using only the best quality and heart-healthy ingredients, you'll find that you'll have better health, more energy and a newly developed taste for good food.

Breakfasts

SOY YOGURT AND COCOA PLUMCAKE (NO EGGS AND NO BUTTER)

Servings: 6-8

Cooking Time: 30 min

- 3 cup of whole wheat flour
- 2 cup white soy yogurt (low in sugar)
- 2 tbsp of stevia powder
- 3 tbsp of rice oil
- 2 tbsp of bitter cocoa powder
- One sachet of baking powder
- Grated orange peel to taste

Directions:

1. First of all, preheat the oven (static) to 350°F and line a 30 cm rectangular plumcake mold with a sheet of baking paper;
2. In a large bowl, pour the sifted flour, stevia, cocoa powder, grated orange peel and baking powder; then mix;
3. Add the yogurt and oil to the mixture and mix well with a kitchen spoon;
4. Once the mixture is smooth and free of lumps, pour it into the plumcake mold and bake at 350F for about 30 minutes; once cooked, it is recommended to let the plumcake cool; portion and serve.

Per Serving:

Calories: 220; Total Fat: 8,8g; Saturated Fat: 2g; Cholesterol: 1mg; Total Carbs: 49g; Fiber: 3g; Protein: 6g

HONEY CAKES

Servings: 4

Cooking Time: 30 min

- 1¼ cups almond milk
- 1 cup oats and honey granola
- 2 tbsp sunflower oil, divided
- 2 large free-range eggs
- 1 tsp vanilla extract
- ½ cup whole-wheat flour
- 1 tbsp organic honey, plus extra for garnish
- 1 tsp baking powder
- ¼ tsp Himalayan pink salt
- 2 medium bananas, mashed

Directions:

1. Add the almond milk, oats and honey granola, 1 tablespoon sunflower oil, 2 large eggs, and vanilla extract to a large bowl. Mix until well incorporated. Add the whole wheat flour, organic honey, baking powder and Himalayan pink salt. Mix until it reaches the consistency of a batter.

2. Heat a large crepe pan over medium heat. Add the remaining tablespoon of sunflower oil and tilt to coat the bottom.
3. Add ¼ cup of batter per griddlecake. Cook for 2 to 3 minutes. Once the tops are bubbly and the bottoms are golden, flip, and cook for 2 minutes, or until golden.
4. Serve warm with mashed banana and a drizzle of honey.

Per Serving:

Calories: 273; Total Fat: 12g; Saturated Fat: 2g; Cholesterol: 97mg; Sodium: 339mg; Total Carbs: 32g; Fiber: 4g; Protein: 10g

---

VEGETABLE SHAKE

Servings: 2

Preparation Time: 8 min

- 2 cups carrots, chopped
- 2 cups kale, chopped
- 2 cups cashew milk
- 2 tbsp ground flaxseed
- 1 (1½-inch) piece of fresh ginger, peeled
- ½ cup ice

Directions:

1. Add the chopped carrots, chopped kale, cashew milk, ground flaxseed, and peeled ginger to a blender.
2. Mix for 1 to 3 minutes, or until completely smooth with no lumps.
3. Add the ice and blend until smooth. Serve cold.

Per Serving:

Calories: 139; Total Fat: 8g; Saturated Fat: 0g; Sodium: 210mg; Total Carbs: 16g; Fiber: 7g; Protein: 5g

---

VEGGIE EGG MUFFINS

Servings: 4

Cooking Time: 20 min

- Cooking spray
- 4 eggs
- 2 tablespoons unsweetened rice milk
- ½ sweet onion, chopped
- ½ red bell pepper, chopped
- A pinch of red pepper flakes
- A pinch of ground black pepper

Directions:

1. Preheat the oven to 350f.
2. Spray 4 muffin pans with cooking spray. Set aside.
3. Whisk together the milk, eggs, onion, red pepper, parsley, red pepper flakes, and black pepper until mixed.
4. Pour the egg mixture into prepared muffin pans.
5. Bake until the muffins are puffed and golden, about 18 to 20 minutes. Serve.

Per Serving:

Calories: 84; Total Fat: 5g; Saturated Fat: 2,3g; Sodium: 438mg; Total Carbs: 3,6g; Fiber: 0,8g; Protein: 10,6g

---

QUICK & CRUNCHY STRAWBERRY OATS

Servings: 4

Cooking Time: 60 min

- ½ cup raw old-fashioned oats
- 1 cup almond milk
- ½ tsp. ground cinnamon
- 2 tsp. raw wild honey
- ¼ cup store-bought crunchy granola
- 1 cup fresh strawberries, sliced

Directions:

1. In an airtight container with a fitted lid, whisk the raw oats and almond milk. Seal the container, and chill overnight or for a minimum of 8 hours.
2. Whisk the cinnamon and honey into the chilled oats when ready to serve. Spoon the oats into two separate bowls, and top with granola and strawberries.
3. Serve immediately, and enjoy!

Per Serving:

Calories: 178; Total Fat: 6g; Saturated Fat: 1,4g; Sodium: 30mg; Total Carbs: 25g; Sugar: 12g; Fiber: 2g; Protein: 4g

---

MEDITERRANEAN EGG SCRAMBLE

Servings: 4

Cooking Time: 60 min

- 10 halved cherry tomatoes
- 4 eggs, beaten
- 2 tsp chopped fresh oregano
- 1 tbsp extra-virgin olive oil
- ½ garlic clove, sliced
- ½ avocado, sliced

Directions:

1. Mix the eggs and oregano in a medium bowl. Warm the olive oil in a large nonstick skillet over medium heat.
2. Scramble the eggs with a wide spatula after pouring them in.
3. Transfer the eggs to a serving dish. Add the cherry tomatoes and garlic to the pan and sauté for about 2 minutes.
4. Spoon the tomatoes over the eggs and top the dish with the avocado slices. Serve right away and enjoy!

Per Serving:

Calories: 199; Total Fat: 12g; Saturated Fat: 2,6g; Sodium: 355mg; Total Carbs: 3,5g; Sugar: 1,4g; Protein: 8,5g

FRUITY BREAKFAST COUSCOUS

Servings: 4

Cooking Time: 15 min

- 1 cinnamon stick
- 3 cups low fat milk
- ¼ tsp. Himalayan salt
- 2 tbsp. raw honey (extra for serving)
- ¼ cup dried raisins
- ½ cup dried apricots, chopped
- 1 cup raw whole-wheat couscous
- 4 tsp. melted butter

Directions:

1. Place the cinnamon stick, along with the milk, in a medium-sized saucepan over medium-high heat, and heat until just under a simmer. The milk should simmer gently but not boil.
2. Transfer the pot to a wooden chopping board, and gently whisk in the salt, honey, raisins, apricots, and couscous. Place a lid on pot and allow the mixture to stand for about 15 minutes, or until the couscous has softened.
3. Divide the couscous between four bowls, and serve topped with 1 teaspoon of butter per bowl and extra honey if desired.

Per Serving:

Calories: 333; Total Fat: 8g; Saturated Fat: 5g; Carbohydrates: 54g; Protein: 12g; Sodium: 266mg; Fiber: 3g

ZESTY FRUIT PARFAITS

Servings: 4

Preparation Time: 5 min

- 2 cups reduced-fat plain Greek yogurt
- 1 tsp. pure vanilla essence
- 2 tbsp. chia seeds
- 2 tsp. finely grated lemon zest
- 2 tbsp. fresh lemon juice
- ¼ cup raw honey
- 1 cup fresh blueberries
- 1 cup fresh strawberries, halved

Directions:

1. In a mid-sized bowl, whisk together the yogurt, vanilla, chia seeds, lemon zest, lemon juice, and honey.
2. Divide half of the yogurt mixture between four serving bowls, followed by 1/2 cup of blueberries and strawberries. Repeat the same process with the remaining yogurt and fruit.
3. Serve immediately.

Per Serving:

Calories: 214g; Total Fat: 4g; Saturated Fat: 2g; Carbohydrates: 33g; Protein: 13g; Sodium: 48mg; Fiber: 5g

---

SALMON & SWISS CHARD CREPES

Servings: 2

Cooking Time: 15 min

- 1 cup fresh Swiss chard, chopped
- 1 tbsp. flax meal
- 1 tbsp. nutritional yeast
- ¼ tsp. crushed dried thyme
- 1 small bunch of fresh parsley, chopped
- Himalayan salt
- Freshly ground black pepper
- 2 large free-range eggs
- 2 tsp. extra-virgin olive oil
- 3 oz. wild smoked salmon
- ½ large Hass avocado, sliced
- 2 tbsp. feta, crumbled
- 1 tsp. fresh lemon juice

Directions:

1. Combine the Swiss chard, flax meal, nutritional yeast, thyme, and parsley in a blender. Add a pinch of salt and pepper to taste before pulsing the mixture until the chard is fine. Add the eggs and combine until the mixture just comes together.
2. 1 teaspoon olive oil, heated in a large frying pan over medium heat. Add half of the chard mixture to the hot oil and gently stir the pan around until the mixture is evenly distributed on the bottom. Fry for about 3 minutes, or until the crepe is no longer jiggly but not completely firm.
3. Top the crepe with half of the salmon, avocado, and feta. Drizzle the whole crepe with 1 teaspoon lemon juice while still in the pan. Transfer the crêpe carefully to a plate, and keep warm while you repeat the process with the remaining ingredients.
4. Serve the crepes warm, and enjoy.

Per Serving:

Calories: 679; Total Fat: 49.2g; Saturated Fat: 11.6g; Carbohydrates: 6.6g; Protein: 44.4g; Fiber: 12.7g

---

SPINACH WRAPS

Servings: 2

Cooking Time: 15 min

- 3 large eggs
- 2 large whole-grain tortillas
- 4 Cheddar cheese slices
- 2 cups spinach, divided
- 1 medium tomato, chopped, divided
- 2 tbsp Tomato Salsa, divided
- 1 tbsp avocado oil

Directions:

1. Crack the eggs into a large bowl. Beat gently with a fork.
2. Set out two plates and place a whole-wheat tortilla on each. Place 2 cheddar cheese slices down the middle of each tortilla. Top each with half of the spinach, then half of the tomato and tomato salsa.
3. Heat the avocado oil in a nonstick frying over medium heat. Add the beaten eggs and stir occasionally until they are scrambled.
4. Once the eggs are done, spoon them on top of the tomatoes and salsa.
5. Gently fold in the sides of the tortillas and roll them up.
6. Place the wraps, seam-side down, in the pan, cover, and warm through for 2 to 3 minutes over medium heat, watching that they don't burn. Serve warm.

Per Serving:

Calories: 471; Total Fat: 27g; Saturated Fat: 8g; Cholesterol: 300mg; Sodium: 627mg; Total Carbs:35g; Fiber: 8g; Protein: 22g

HONEY-SWEETENED GREEK YOGURT

Servings: 2-3

Cooking Time: 0 min

- 1/3 tsp. pure vanilla essence
- 2 cups plain Greek yogurt
- ¼ cup raw honey
- 1/3 tsp. ground nutmeg
- 1 cup blueberries

Directions:

1. Whisk together the vanilla and yogurt in a medium glass bowl. Gradually whisk in a small amount of honey, tasting the sweetness as you go and adding the honey to taste, but not exceeding 1/2 a cup. Once the yogurt is sweetened to your liking, whisk in the nutmeg.
2. Scrape the yogurt into serving bowls, and garnish with the blueberries before serving.

Per Serving:

Calories: 295; Total Fat: 11g; Saturated Fat: 5.5 g; Carbohydrates: 55g; Protein: 23g; Sodium: 82mg; Fiber: 2g

SAVORY MUSHROOM PANCAKES

Servings: 2

Cooking Time: 20 min

- ½ cup almond milk
- ½ cup chickpea flour
- 6 tbsp. extra-virgin olive oil (divided)
- Himalayan salt
- 8 oz. button mushrooms, stems removed
- 3 fresh thyme sprigs
- Freshly ground black pepper
- 1 bunch Swiss chard, ribs removed, finely chopped

Directions:

1. Whisk together the flour, milk, 2 tablespoons olive oil, and a small pinch of salt in a medium-sized mixing bowl until you have a nearly smooth batter. Set the batter aside to rest for 15 minutes while you prepare the rest of the dish.
2. Heat 1 tblsp of olive oil in a large skillet over medium heat. When the oil is nice and hot, add the mushrooms, thyme, 1/8 teaspoon of salt, and a pinch of black pepper. Fry the mushrooms for about 5 minutes or until they darken. Scrape the cooked mushrooms into a bowl, and keep warm.
3. Heat 1 tbsp of oil in the same skillet, and add the chard, along with another 1/8 teaspoon salt and an extra pinch of black pepper. Fry the chard for about 5 minutes, or until all the leaves have wilted. Scrape the cooked chard into the same bowl with the mushrooms, and keep warm.
4. Use a crumpled piece of baking paper to wipe vegetables and excess oil from the skillet. Add 1 tbsp of oil to the skillet and return to medium heat. When the oil is hot, beat the batter once more to incorporate as much air as possible. Add half of the batter to the hot oil, gently swirling the skillet to coat the bottom. Fry the pancake for 2-3 minutes before flipping and frying the other side until lightly browned – about 2-3 minutes. Repeat with the remaining oil and batter and flip the pancake onto a plate.
5. Serve the pancakes warm and topped with cooked mushrooms and chard.

Per Serving:

Calories: 530; Total Fat: 45g; Saturated Fat: 7,5g; Total Carbs: 26g; Protein: 11g; Sodium: 490mg; Fiber: 10g

---

YOGURT-TOPPED SQUASH FRITTERS

Servings: 4-6

Cooking Time: 10 min

- 6 small yellow squash, grated
- 1 ¼ tsp. Himalayan salt (divided)
- ½ lemon, juiced
- 2 tsp. sweet smoked paprika
- 1 cup plain Greek yogurt
- ¼ tsp. white pepper
- ½ cup all-purpose flour
- 3 large free-range eggs, beaten
- 4 spring onions, thinly sliced
- ¼ cup fresh parsley, finely chopped
- 4 oz. feta cheese, crumbled
- olive oil for frying

Directions:

1. Toss the grated squash in a large bowl with 1 teaspoon of salt. Transfer to a colander set over the sink and drain for at least 20 minutes. Use a wooden spoon or ladle's back to gently press any excess water from the vegetables before transferring them back to a bowl.
2. Whisk the lemon juice, paprika, yogurt, and 1/4 teaspoon of salt in a medium glass bowl. Set aside.
3. Add the pepper, flour, eggs, spring onions, parsley, and crumbled feta to the bowl with the squash, gently stirring to combine.
4. In a medium frying saucepan over medium-high heat, heat 1/2-inch of oil. Test the oil by inserting the tip of a toothpick – the oil is ready when the toothpick immediately begins to sizzle. Place the batter into the hot oil with a spoon, roughly 4-5 fritters at a time. Lightly flatten the fritters with a spatula, and fry for 2 minutes. Cook for an additional 2 minutes on the opposite side, or until both sides are lightly browned.
5. Transfer the cooked fritters to a serving platter, and keep warm.
6. Serve the fritters warm, topped with the yogurt dressing.

Per Serving:

Calories: 237; Total Fat: 14g; Saturated fat: 2g; Total Carbs: 18g; Protein: 11g; Sodium: 655mg; Fiber: 3g

CHEESY, ALMOND-CRUSTED CHARD PIE

Servings: 16

Cooking Time: 1 hour

- 3 tbsp. cool water
- 1 tbsp. flaxseed meal (plus 2 tsp.)
- Freshly ground black pepper
- 1/8 tsp. kosher salt (plus 1/4 tsp.)
- ½ tsp. dried oregano
- 1 cup almond flour
- 1 tbsp. avocado oil
- 1 tbsp. extra-virgin olive oil
- 2 tsp. crushed garlic
- ½ medium shallot, finely chopped
- 10 oz. Swiss chard
- ½ tsp. dried oregano
- 5 oz. soft goat cheese, grated
- 2 large free-range eggs
- 1/4 cup almond slivers

Directions:

1. Set the oven to preheat to 350F, with the wire rack in the center of the oven. Set aside a large casserole dish that has been sprayed with baking spray.
2. Place the water in a medium-sized bowl, along with the flaxseed meal, and gently combine. Lightly beat in a pinch of freshly ground black pepper, along with the salt, oregano, and almond flour. Add the oil, and mix until the ingredients come together to form a dough. Use your hands to gather the dough together and press it tightly into the prepared casserole dish. Press up the sides, as well, to form a rim. Bake the crust in the oven for about 18 minutes or until golden brown.
3. Meanwhile, heat the olive oil in a big pot over medium-low heat. When the oil is hot, fry the garlic and shallots for about 5 minutes or until the shallots are tender and translucent. Stir in the chard, and fry for about 2 minutes, until the chard has reduced in size.
4. Transfer the pot to a wooden chopping board, and stir in the remaining 1/4 teaspoon of salt, a large pinch of pepper, oregano, cheese, and eggs.
5. Pour the filling into the pre-baked crust, sprinkle with the almond slivers before returning the pie to the oven and baking for another 28 minutes, or until the filling is firm and the almonds are lightly toasted.
6. Slice, and serve hot, or chill for a tasty snack.

Per Serving:

Calories: 113; Total Fat: 9g; Saturated Fat: 2,4g; Total Carbs: 3g; Protein: 5g; Sodium: 122g; Fiber: 2g

---

OLIVE-STUFFED CHICKEN BREASTS

Servings: 8-10

Cooking Time: 4 min

- 2 tbsp. balsamic vinegar
- 1 tbsp. extra-virgin olive oil
- 4 tsp. crushed garlic
- ¼ cup roasted sweet red peppers, drained
- 4 green olives, pitted

- 4 Spanish olives, pitted
- 4 black olives
- 4 oil-packed sun-dried tomatoes
- 4 boneless chicken breasts, skins removed
- Grated Parmesan cheese for garnishing

Directions:

1. In a blender, pulse the vinegar, oil, garlic, sweet peppers, olives, and tomatoes on medium, until you have a lumpy paste.
2. Slice the chicken breasts open, taking care not to cut all the way through. Divide the olive paste between the breasts and use a spoon to fill each one.
3. Close the breasts with toothpicks to ensure the filling doesn't come out.
4. Place the stuffed breasts on a lightly coated rack, and broil in the oven on high for 9-11 minutes, or until the chicken is properly cooked. Keep an eye on the chicken to ensure it doesn't burn.

5. Remove the toothpicks and serve hot, garnished with the cheese.

Per Serving:

Calories: 264; Total Fat: 11g; Saturated Fat: 2g; Total Carbs: 5g; Protein: 35g; Sodium: 367mg; Fiber: 1g

---

SPICY CRAB BITES

Servings: 30

Cooking Time: 12 min

- 30 miniature, frozen phyllo tart shells
- ½ tsp. seafood seasoning
- ½ cup reduced-fat spreadable garden vegetable cream cheese
- ½ tsp. freshly ground black pepper
- 1/3 tsp. cayenne pepper
- 1/3 cup lump crab meat, drained
- 5 tbsp. hot sauce

Directions:

1. Cook the miniature tart shells according to package instructions and cool completely on a wire rack.
2. Whisk the seafood seasoning, cream cheese, black pepper, and cayenne pepper in a medium-sized mixing bowl. Gently stir in the crab meat until all ingredients are properly combined.
3. Spoon the mixture into the cooled phyllo shells, and top with a few splashes of hot sauce before serving.

Per Serving:

Calories: 34; Total Fat: 2g; Saturated Fat: 0g; Total Carbs: 3g; Protein: 1g; Sodium: 103mg; Fiber: 0g

---

ROAST BEEF & ASPARAGUS BUNDLES

Servings: 3

Cooking Time: 16 min

- 16 fresh asparagus spears, trimmed
- 1/8 tsp. ground cumin
- 1 tsp. lemon juice
- 1 tsp. French mustard
- 1 tsp. crushed garlic
- 1/3 cup mayonnaise
- 8 thin slices of deli roast beef, cut in half lengthwise
- 3 different colored medium sweet peppers, thinly sliced

- 16 whole chives
- Freshly ground black pepper

Directions:

1. Bring a small saucepan of water to a boil over high heat. When the water is boiling, add the asparagus spears, and cook for 3 minutes. Strain the asparagus spears immediately after cooking, and place them in a bowl of ice water. Strain again, and pat completely dry.
2. Whisk the cumin, lemon juice, mustard, garlic, and mayonnaise in a small glass bowl.
3. Lay the roast beef slices out over a clean work surface. Top each slice of roast beef with 1 teaspoon of the mayonnaise mixture, using the back of the teaspoon to spread it out. Place 1 asparagus spear on each beef slice, and top with slices of each color sweet pepper. Sprinkle with black pepper before rolling up the bundles and securing them with the chive strands.
4. Serve immediately.

Per Serving:

Calories: 52; Total Fat: 4g; Saturated Fat: 1g; Carbohydrates: 2g; Protein: 2g; Sodium: 74mg; Fiber: 1g

LEMON GRILLED OYSTERS

Servings: 4

Cooking Time: 10 min

- 24 fresh oysters in their shells
- Flaky sea salt
- White pepper
- ½ lime, juiced

Directions:

1. Set the grill to preheat on high.
2. With the flattest side against the grill, cook the oysters for 5-10 minutes or until they open.
3. Crack off the top half of each oyster shell, leaving the oysters in the bottom half.
4. Transfer the grilled oysters to a serving platter. Season the oysters to taste with salt and pepper. Drizzle the lime juice evenly over the oysters, and serve straight away.

Quick Tip: Discard any oysters that have opened before cooking, as this means they are not safe to eat.

Per Serving (3 oysters):

Calories: 61; Total Fat: 5,1g; Saturated Fat: 2,9g; Total Carbs: 1,5g; Protein: 2,5g; Sodium: 55mg; Fiber: 0,1g

PEANUT BUTTER BITES

Servings: 24

Cooking Time: 0 min

- 3/4 tsp. Himalayan salt
- 1 tbsp. pure vanilla essence
- 3 tbsp. coconut milk
- 6 tbsp. coconut sugar
- ½ cup natural peanut butter

- 15 oz. canned no-salt-added chickpeas drained and rinsed
- 1 ½ cups old-fashioned rolled oats
- 2/3 cup dark chocolate chips

Directions:

1. In a high-powered blender, pulse the salt, vanilla, coconut milk, coconut sugar, peanut butter, and chickpeas on high until you have a lump-free mixture. You may want to take a break from time to time to scrape the sides of the blender. The process should take about 1-2 minutes.
2. Gradually add 1 cup of oats to the blender, pulsing and scraping the sides, until you, once again, have a lump-free batter. Scrape the mixture into a medium-sized bowl, and stir in the remaining oats and the chocolate chips.
3. Roll the mixture into 24 balls of roughly the same size. Arrange the balls on a baking sheet and chill, covered in cling wrap, for at least 1 hour.
4. Serve the peanut butter bites chilled.

Quick Tip: The bites can also be frozen in an airtight container. Use greaseproof paper to separate the bites while freezing. Allow the bites to defrost at room temperature for 10 minutes to serve.

Per Serving (1 bite):

Calories: 201; Total Fat: 12g; Saturated Fat: 3g; Total Carbs: 16g; Protein: 6g; Sodium: 69mg; Fiber: 4g

---

CORIANDER & LIME AVOCADO HUMMUS

Servings: 4

Cooking Time: 0 min

- 3 tbsp. filtered water
- ½ tsp. crushed red pepper (optional)
- ¼ tsp. freshly ground black pepper
- ¼ tsp. Himalayan salt

- ½ tsp. ground cumin
- 1 tsp. crushed garlic
- 3 tbsp. freshly squeezed lime juice
- ¼ cup fresh coriander leaves, chopped

- 1 small ripe avocado, pitted and peeled
- 2 tbsp. extra-virgin olive oil

- 15 oz. canned no-salt-added chickpeas drained and rinsed

Directions:

1. Place all ingredients in a high-powered blender, and pulse on high until you have a smooth paste. You will need to pause now and then to scrape down the sides of the blender. If the hummus is too thick, add more filtered water, 1 tablespoon at a time, until you have the desired consistency.
2. Scrape the hummus into a serving bowl and chill, covered with cling wrap, until ready to serve.

Per Serving (0,25 cups):

Calories: 96; Total Fat: 5g; Saturated Fat: 1,2g; Total Carbs: 10g; Protein: 4g; Fiber: 3g

---

OVEN-BAKED SPINACH CHIPS

Servings: 4

Cooking Time: 15 min

- 2 lbs. savoy spinach
- ½ tsp. kosher salt

- 3 tbsp. extra-virgin olive oil

Directions:

1. Set the oven to preheat to 375°F, with the wire rack in the center of the oven, and line a large, rimmed baking tray with greaseproof paper.
2. Use a sharp knife to remove the spinach stems, and cut the larger leaves down to roughly the same size.
3. Toss the ingredients together in a large mixing bowl spinach leaves with salt and olive oil until all the leaves are evenly coated and seasoned.
4. Arrange the seasoned spinach on the prepared baking tray, and bake in the oven until the leaves are crispy about 15 minutes.
5. Let the chips cool on the counter before serving.

Per Serving (134g):

Calories: 147; Total Fat: 14g; Saturated Fat: 1,9g; Total Carbs: 4g; Protein: 3g; Fiber: 2,6g

AVOCADO, CHERRY TOMATOES AND TOFU SALAD

Servings: 4

Cooking Time: 0 min

- 14 oz natural tofu
- 2 avocados
- 1 cup cherry tomatoes

- 2 tablespoons of extra virgin olive oil
- Salt to taste

Directions:

1. First, it is best to drain the tofu, rinse it and blot the water with a sheet of kitchen paper; then, cut the tofu into cubes.
2. Wash the cherry tomatoes in water and bicarbonate of soda, then cut them into slices; clean the avocados by removing the skin and stone, then cut the flesh into cubes.
3. Pour all ingredients into a large bowl, add the indicated amount of oil and a small amount of salt; then mix, portion and serve.

Per Serving:

Calories 130; Protein 1.7g; Carbohydrates 7.2g; Fiber 3.4g; Sugars 2.4g; Fat 11.5g; Saturated fat 1.6g; Sodium 114.8mg

---

SWEET POTATO, RADICCHIO AND CHIA SEED SALAD

Servings: 4

Cooking Time: 5/10 min

- 21 oz sweet potatoes
- 14 oz red radicchio
- 3 tbsp of extra virgin olive oil

- 3 tbsp of chia seeds
- Salt to taste

Directions:

1. Peel and thinly slice the sweet potatoes before grilling them for a few minutes.
2. Clean and wash the radicchio in plenty of water and bicarbonate of soda.

3. Combine the vegetables in a large bowl, adding the indicated amount of olive oil, chia seeds (previously soaked for 10 minutes), and a small amount of salt. Then mix the ingredients, portion and serve.

Per Serving:

Calories: 254kcal; Carbohydrates: 25g; Protein: 4g; Fat: 16g; Saturated Fat: 2g; Sodium: 630mg; Fiber: 5g; Sugar: 8g

---

GRANNY SMITH SALAD

Servings: 2

Preparation Time: 10 min

- 1 tbsp organic apple cider vinegar
- 1 tbsp avocado oil
- 2 tsp organic honey
- 4 cups red cabbage, cut into bite-size pieces

- 2 Granny Smith apples, core removed and cut into thin slices
- Ground black pepper

Directions:

1. In a wide sized mixing bowl, add the apple cider vinegar, avocado oil, and organic honey, mix to combine.
2. Add the cut cabbage and sliced apples in the same mixing bowl and mix to combine.
3. Season with ground black pepper to taste. Serve immediately.

Per Serving:

Calories: 176; Total Fat: 7g; Saturated Fat: 1g; Cholesterol: 0mg; Sodium: 34mg; Total Carbs: 28g; Fiber: 6g; Protein: 3g

---

ARUGULA SALAD

Servings: 4

Cooking Time: 60 min

- 1 large brown onion, cut into crescents and separated
- 1 tbsp balsamic vinegar
- 1 tsp whole grain mustard

- 1 tbsp avocado oil
- 1 red bell pepper, seeds removed and cut into strips
- ¼ tsp ground black pepper

- 4 cups baby arugula

Directions:

1. Set an oven rack beneath the broiler and preheat on high. Line a baking sheet with aluminum foil.
2. Place the crescent onions and sliced red bell pepper onto the baking sheet and coat with balsamic vinegar. Spread the vegetables on the baking sheet. Broil for 10 minutes until crispy and slightly browned.
3. In a small-sized mixing bowl, add the whole grain mustard, avocado oil, and ground black pepper, mix to combine.
4. Place the baby arugula on a large serving plate to create a bed, top with the roasted onion and bell pepper mixture, and drizzle with the mustard dressing. Serve immediately.

Per Serving:

Calories: 127; Total Fat: 7g; Saturated Fat: 1g; Cholesterol: 0mg; Sodium: 115mg; Total Carbs: 14g; Fiber: 4g; Protein: 3g

COUSCOUS SALAD

Servings: 2

Cooking Time: 15 min

- ½ cup couscous
- 1 cup water
- 1 cup sugar snap peas

- 2 tbsp roasted sesame dressing
- 1 ½ cup carrots, peeled and grated
- 2 cups red cabbage, thinly sliced

Directions:

1. In a small-sized stockpot, bring the couscous and water to a boil. Bring the heat down to low, cover, and allow simmering for 8 minutes.
2. Add the sugar snap peas to the pot and cook for 4 minutes until the water has been absorbed and the sugar snap peas are tender.
3. In a wide sized mixing bowl, add the cooked couscous and sugar snap peas mixture, sesame dressing, grated carrots, and sliced cabbage, mix to combine and serve warm or cold.

Per Serving:

Calories: 231; Total Fat: 7g; Saturated Fat: 1g; Cholesterol: 0mg; Sodium: 69mg; Total Carbs: 47g; Fiber: 11g; Protein: 18g

BRUSSELS SPROUT AND APPLE SLAW

Servings: 4

Preparation Time: 15 min

- 1 pound (454 g) Brussels sprouts, stem ends removed and sliced thinly

Dressing:

- 1 teaspoon Dijon mustard
- 2 teaspoons apple cider vinegar
- 1 tablespoon raw honey

For Garnish:

- ½ cup pomegranate seeds

- 1 apple, cored and sliced thinly
- ½ red onion, sliced thinly

- 1 cup plain coconut yogurt
- 1 teaspoon sea salt

- ½ cup chopped toasted hazelnuts

Directions:

1. Mix the ingredients for the salad in a large salad bowl, then toss to combine well.
2. Mix the ingredients for the dressing in a small bowl, then stir to mix well.
3. Dress the salad let it sit for 10 minutes. Serve with pomegranate seeds and toasted hazelnuts on top.

Per Serving:

Calories: 248; Fat: 11.2g; Saturated Fat: 0,7g; Protein: 12.7g; Total Carbs: 29.9g; Sugar: 12g; Fiber: 8.0g; Sodium: 645mg

TUNA SALAD

Servings: 4

Preparation Time: 8 min

- 1 tsp. Himalayan salt
- 3 tbsp. white wine vinegar
- 1/4 cup extra-virgin olive oil
- 1 tsp. crushed garlic

- 1 red bell pepper, seeded and diced
- 1 cup pitted green olives
- 6 oz. canned tuna in olive oil, well-drained
- 1 bag mixed salad greens

Directions:

1. Place the salt, vinegar, and oil in a large mixing bowl. Whisk until properly combined.

2. Gently stir in the garlic, bell peppers, and olives. Add the drained tuna, and stir until all ingredients are properly combined. Seal the bowl, and chill for a minimum of 1 hour.
3. Serve the chilled tuna mixture on a bed of mixed salad greens

Per Serving:

Calories: 343; Total Fat: 28g; Saturated Fat: 4g; Carbohydrates: 6g; Protein: 21g; Sodium: 1,217mg; Fiber: 2g

FRESH MINT & TOASTED PITA SALAD

Servings: 4

Cooking Time: 60 min

- 1/4 tsp. freshly ground black pepper
- 1/2 tsp. ground sumac (extra for garnish)
- 1 tsp. Himalayan salt
- 1 tsp. crushed garlic
- 1/2 cup extra-virgin olive oil
- 1/2 cup freshly squeezed lemon juice
- 2 whole-wheat pita bread rounds, toasted, and broken into bite-sized pieces
- 1 bunch spring onions, thinly sliced
- 1 small green bell pepper, diced
- 1/4 cup fresh mint leaves, chopped
- 1/2 cup fresh parsley, chopped
- 2 heirloom tomatoes, diced
- 2 small English cucumbers, diced
- 2 cups romaine lettuce, shredded

Directions:

1. Whisk together the pepper, sumac, salt, garlic, olive oil, and lemon juice in a glass bowl. Set aside.
2. Toss together the toasted pita bites, spring onions, bell pepper, mint, parsley, tomatoes, cucumbers, and shredded lettuce in a mixing bowl. Drizzle the olive oil dressing, and serve immediately, garnished with the extra ground sumac.

Per Serving:

Calories: 359; Total Fat: 27g; Saturated Fat: 4g; Carbohydrates: 29g; Protein: 6g; Sodium: 777mg; Fiber: 6g

ZESTY VINAIGRETTE POTATO SALAD

Servings: 12

Cooking Time: 20 min

- 3 lbs. red potatoes, cubed
- 1/4 tsp. freshly ground black pepper

- 1 1/2 tsp. Himalayan salt
- 2 tbsp. balsamic vinegar
- 2 tbsp. freshly squeezed lemon juice
- 1/3 cup extra-virgin olive oil
- 1/2 tsp. dried oregano

- 1 tsp. crushed garlic
- 2 tbsp. fresh parsley, finely chopped
- 1/3 cup red onion, chopped
- 1/2 cup Greek olives, pitted and chopped
- 1/2 cup parmesan cheese, grated

Directions:

1. Cover the potatoes with water in a pot over medium-high heat and bring to a rolling boil. Once the water has reached a boil, reduce the heat to low and cook for 10-15 minutes, or until the potatoes are fork-tender. In a colander over the sink, wash the cooked potatoes.
2. In a glass bowl, whisk the pepper, salt, vinegar, lemon juice, and oil until all ingredients are properly combined. Add the garlic, oregano and parsley, and stir to combine.
3. Place the drained potatoes in a large bowl, and toss together with the onions, olives, and dressing. Refrigerate for at least two hours after covering the bowl.
4. Stir in the cheese right before serving, and enjoy.

Per Serving:

Calories: 168; Total Fat: 9g; Saturated Fat: 2g; Carbohydrates: 20g; Protein: 4g; Sodium: 451mg; Fiber: 2g

PARMESAN PEAR SALAD

Servings: 4

Cooking Time: 60 min

For the dressing:

- 3 tbsp avocado oil
- 2 tsp whole grain mustard

- 2 tsp cooking sherry
- 2 tsp apple cider vinegar

For the salad:

- 1 head Romaine lettuce, torn into pieces
- 2 bartlett pears, cored and cut into bite-size pieces

- ¼ cup salted sunflower seeds
- ½ cup Parmesan cheese, grated
- Ground black pepper

Directions:

For the dressing:

1. Add the avocado oil, whole grain mustard, cooking sherry, apple cider vinegar, and whisk to combine in a wide mixing bowl.

For the salad:

1. Add the Romaine lettuce leaves and pear pieces into the bowl and toss the dressing until well coated.
2. Sprinkle with the sunflower seeds, grated Parmesan cheese, and a ground black pepper. Serve cold.

Per Serving:

Calories: 244; Total Fat: 17g; Saturated Fat: 4g; Cholesterol: 7mg; Sodium: 219mg; Total Carbs: 18g; Fiber: 4g; Protein: 7g

---

FRESH MINT & TOASTED PITA SALAD

Servings: 4

Cooking Time: 0 min

- 1/4 tsp. freshly ground black pepper
- 1/2 tsp. ground sumac (extra for garnish)
- 1 tsp. Himalayan salt
- 1 tsp. crushed garlic
- 1/2 cup extra-virgin olive oil
- 1/2 cup freshly squeezed lemon juice
- 2 whole-wheat pita bread rounds, toasted and broken into bite-sized pieces

- 1 bunch spring onions, thinly sliced
- 1 small green bell pepper, diced
- 1/4 cup fresh mint leaves, chopped
- 1/2 cup fresh parsley, chopped
- 2 heirloom tomatoes, diced
- 2 small English cucumbers, diced
- 2 cups romaine lettuce, shredded

Directions:

1. Whisk together the pepper, sumac, salt, garlic, olive oil, and lemon juice in a glass bowl. Set aside.
2. Toss together the toasted pita bites, spring onions, bell pepper, mint, parsley, tomatoes, cucumbers, and shredded lettuce in a wide mixing bowl. Drizzle the olive oil dressing, and serve immediately, garnished with the extra ground sumac.

Per Serving:

Calories: 359; Total Fat: 27g; Saturated Fat: 4g; Carbohydrates: 29g; Protein: 6g; Sodium: 777mg; Fiber: 6g

Soups & Stews

MEXICAN SPICED CHICKEN SOUP

Servings: 6

Cooking Time: 6-8 hours

- 1 tsp. kosher salt
- ½ tsp. white pepper
- 2 tsp. sweet smoked paprika
- 2 tsp. ground cumin
- 1 tbsp. chili powder
- ¼ cup fresh coriander leaves, chopped (extra for garnish)
- 2 cups chicken stock
- 1 tbsp. freshly squeezed lime juice (extra for serving)

- 2 tsp. crushed garlic
- 2 bell peppers, chopped
- 1 ½ cups frozen corn
- 14.5 oz. fire-roasted tomatoes
- 15 oz. canned black turtle beans drained and rinsed
- 1 ½ lbs. boneless chicken breasts, skins removed
- Avocado, diced, for serving

Directions:

1. Stir together the salt, pepper, paprika, cumin, chili powder, coriander leaves, stock, lime juice, garlic, peppers, corn, tomatoes, and black beans in a large slow cooker. Stir in the chicken breasts once all of the ingredients have been thoroughly mixed. Lid the cooker and cook on low for 6-8 hours, or until the chicken is cooked through.
2. Shred the meat using a sharp knife when the chicken is properly cooked.
3. Serve the soup topped with sliced avocado and coriander leaves with a few extra squirts of lime juice.

Per Serving:

Calories: 482; Total Fat: 34g; Saturated Fat: 6g; Cholesterol: 66mg; Sodium: 1260mg; Total Carbs: 34g; Fiber: 8g; Protein: 16g

---

BELL PEPPER RICE SOUP

Servings: 8

Cooking Time: 5-6 hours

- 1 ½ tbsp. extra-virgin avocado oil
- 1 small shallot, diced

- 3 tsp. crushed garlic
- 4 cups beef stock

- 1 lb. ground beef
- ¼ tsp. white pepper
- 1 tsp. kosher salt
- 1 tsp. dried dill
- 1 tsp. dried oregano
- 1 tsp. sweet smoked paprika

- 2 cups long-grain brown rice
- 14.5 oz. canned diced tomatoes, with the juices
- 14.4 oz. canned tomato sauce
- 1 green bell pepper, seeded and diced

Directions:

1. In a wide frying saucepan over medium-high heat, heat the avocado oil. Fry the shallots in the heated oil for 3-4 minutes or until they become translucent. Stir in the garlic for 1-2 minutes, allowing the flavors to meld. Pour in the stock, and add the beef, stirring for 3-5 minutes, until the beef is properly cooked.
2. Scrape the beef into a large slow cooker, and stir in the pepper, salt, dill, oregano, paprika, rice, diced tomatoes, tomato sauce, and bell peppers.
3. Place a lid on the cooker, and cook on low for 5-6 hours.
4. Ladle the soup into bowls, and serve hot.

Per Serving:

Calories: 244; Total Fat: 7g; Saturated Fat: 2g; Cholesterol: 32mg; Sodium: 142mg; Total Carbs: 28g; Fiber: 2g; Protein: 21g

---

ITALIAN SPINACH SOUP

Servings: 4

Cooking Time: 30 min

- 2 tbsp. extra-virgin olive oil
- 1 shallot, finely chopped
- 2 tsp. dried oregano
- 1 tsp. kosher salt
- 4 tsp. crushed garlic

- 3 carrots, thinly sliced
- 3 celery stalks, finely chopped
- 1 ½ lbs. ground pork
- 6 cups chicken bone stock
- 1 cup coarsely chopped spinach

Directions:

1. In a wide skillet over medium-high heat, heat the olive oil. When the oil is nice and hot, stir in the shallots, oregano, salt, garlic, carrots, and celery for 5 minutes, or until the vegetables become tender.
2. Stir in the ground pork, and cook for 5-8 minutes, or until the meat is nicely browned.
3. Pour the stock into the pot, and stir to combine. Lower the heat to maintain a gentle simmer when the stock begins to boil for 20 minutes. After 20 minutes, add the spinach, and simmer for a few more minutes until the leaves wilt. If necessary, add more salt to taste.

4. Serve the soup hot.

Quick Tip: Any leftovers can be stored in the fridge in an airtight container for no more than 4 days or frozen for 3 months.

Per Serving:

Calories: 192; Total Fat: 12,6g; Saturated Fat: 5,8g; Total Carbs: 13g; Sugar: 4.3g; Protein: 6,5g

---

VIETNAMESE BEEF SOUP

Servings: 6

Cooking Time: 20 min

- 4 tsp. crushed garlic
- 1 whole cinnamon stick
- 6-inches of fresh ginger, peeled, and halved lengthwise
- 7 oz. packaged shirataki noodles
- 10 cups beef bone stock
- ¼ cup fish sauce
- 2 tsp. pure maple syrup

- 1 tsp. kosher salt
- ¼ cup whole Thai basil leaves
- ¼ cup coriander leaves, chopped
- 2 spring onions, finely chopped
- 1 lb. raw flank steak, finely sliced against the grain
- 1 lime, sliced into 6 wedges

Directions:

1. Stir together the garlic, cinnamon, ginger, noodles, stock, fish sauce, syrup, and salt in a large pot over medium heat. Lower the heat to maintain a slow simmer once the stock begins to boil, and cook covered for 20 minutes, stirring at regular intervals.
2. Discard the ginger, cinnamon, and any small bits floating on the surface.
3. Divide the basil, coriander, spring onions, steak, and noodles between 6 serving bowls. Spoon the hot soup over everything in the bowls; the steak will cook in the soup.
4. Serve the bowls hot, with the lime wedges on the side.

Quick Tip: Any leftovers can be refrigerated in an airtight container for no more than 4 days.

Per Serving:

Calories: 441; Total Fat: 6,2g; Saturated Fat: 2,1g; Total Carbs: 71,4g; Sugar: 8,5g; Protein: 25,1; Fiber: 7,9g; Sodium: 1458mg

CURRIED CHICKPEA STEW

Servings: 5

Cooking Time: 45 min

- 2 tbsp. extra-virgin avocado oil
- 1 medium shallot, diced
- 1-inch fresh ginger, grated
- 2 tsp. crushed garlic
- ½ tsp. kosher salt
- 1 tsp. white pepper
- 1 tsp. ground turmeric
- 15.5 oz. canned chickpeas drained and rinsed
- 2 cups vegetable stock
- 15 oz. canned full-fat coconut milk
- 1 bunch Swiss chard

Directions:

1. Heat the avocado oil in a wide, cast-iron pot over medium heat. When the oil is nice and hot, fry the shallots for 4 minutes or until they become translucent.
2. Stir in the ginger and garlic, allowing the flavors to meld for 2-4 minutes. You may deglaze the pot by adding 1 teaspoon of water at a time, and scraping the food off the bottom with a wooden spoon, if the food is sticking too much.
3. Stir in the salt, pepper, turmeric, and chickpeas for 5-7 minutes, or until the chickpeas get a crispy golden coating.
4. Stir in the stock and coconut milk. Once the stew begins to boil, lower the heat to maintain a gentle simmer for 30-35 minutes or until the stew thickens. Stir at regular intervals to prevent burning.
5. Stir in the chard for 3-6 minutes until the leaves reduce size.
6. Wait for a few minutes of resting time before serving the stew.

Quick Tip: Any leftovers can be refrigerated in an airtight container for no more than 5 days. Let the stew thaw overnight and microwave for 2-3 minutes on high to reheat.

Per Serving:

Calories: 249; Total Fat: 6,5g; Saturated Fat: 1,3g; Sodium: 309mg; Total Carbs: 37,8g; Sugar: 6,7g; Protein: 11,2g; Fiber: 10g; Cholesterol 0.7mg

---

SHRIMP SOUP

Servings: 4

Cooking Time: 45 min

- 1-inch fresh ginger, peeled
- 1 fresh lemongrass stalk, outer layers discarded
- 2 tbsp. freshly squeezed lime juice
- 1 lime, zested
- 4 cups chicken bone stock
- 1 cup button mushrooms, sliced
- 2 tbsp. fresh coriander leaves, chopped
- 1 tsp. pure maple syrup
- 1 tbsp. fish sauce
- 1 cup full-fat unsweetened coconut milk
- 1 lb. shrimp, peeled and deveined

Directions:

1. Lightly smash the ginger and lemongrass with the back of a knife to release the flavors. Chop the lemongrass into 4-inch pieces.
2. In an iron pot over medium heat, bring the ginger, lemongrass, lime juice, lime zest, and chicken stock to a boil. Once the broth is boiling, lower the heat, and simmer for 10 minutes, occasionally stirring to prevent burning. After 10 minutes, discard the ginger and lemongrass, along with any bits floating on the surface.
3. Stir in the mushrooms, and simmer for 25 minutes. Add the coriander leaves, syrup, fish sauce, coconut milk, and shrimp, frying for 4-5 minutes, or until the shrimp blush. Do not overcook the shrimp.
4. Pour the soup into dishes and serve right away.

Quick Tip: Any leftovers can be refrigerated in an airtight container for no more than 4 days.

Per Serving:

Calories: 328; Total Fat: 16g; Saturated Fat: 12,2g; Sodium: 633mg; Total Carbs: 33,8g; Sugar: 6g; Protein: 17,2g; Fiber: 1,5g; Cholesterol 111.3mg

---

CARAMELIZED ONION SOUP

Servings: 4

Cooking Time: 45 min

- ¼ cup extra-virgin avocado oil
- 2 white onions, thinly sliced
- 2 yellow onions, thinly sliced
- 1 tsp. coconut sugar
- 2 fresh thyme sprigs
- 2 whole bay leaves
- 2 tbsp. arrowroot starch
- 6 cups beef bone stock
- Kosher salt
- White pepper

Directions:

1. Heat the avocado oil over medium heat in a large, cast-iron pot. Add the onions, coconut sugar, thyme, and bay leaves, frying for 4 minutes, until the onions become translucent. Stir the onions to caramelize for 20 minutes with the cover on the saucepan, stirring regularly to prevent burning.
2. Drizzle the arrowroot starch over the caramelized onions, and gently whisk in the beef bone stock. Place the lid back on the pot, and simmer for an additional 20 minutes, stirring at regular intervals.
3. Discard the fresh herbs, and season the soup to taste with salt and pepper.

Quick Tip: Any leftovers can be refrigerated in an airtight container for no more than 4 days.

Per Serving:

Calories: 99; Total Fat: 4g; Saturated Fat: 0; Sodium: 540mg; Total Carbs: 10; Sugar: 4g; Protein: 3g; Fiber: 2g; Cholesterol 0mg

---

SWEET PEPPER STEW

Servings: 2

Cooking Time: 50 min

- 2 tablespoons olive oil
- 2 sweet peppers, diced (about 2 cups)
- ½ large onion, minced
- 1 garlic clove, minced
- 1 tablespoon gluten-free Worcestershire sauce
- 1 teaspoon oregano
- 1 cup low-sodium tomato juice
- 1 cup low-sodium vegetable stock
- ¼ cup brown rice
- ¼ cup brown lentils
- Salt to taste

Directions:

1. In a Dutch oven, heat the olive oil over medium-high heat.
2. Sauté the sweet peppers and onion for 10 minutes, stirring occasionally, or until the onion begins to turn golden and the peppers are wilted.
3. Stir in the garlic, Worcestershire sauce, and oregano and cook for 30 seconds more. Add the tomato juice, vegetable stock, rice, and lentils to the Dutch oven and mix well. Heat the mixture to a boil, then decrease to a medium-low heat setting. Let it simmer covered for about 45 minutes, or until the rice is cooked through and the lentils are tender. Sprinkle with salt and serve warm.

Per Serving

Calories: 135; Fat: 7; Saturated Fat: 1,8g; Protein: 8,5; Total Carbs: 32.8g; Fiber: 7.0g; Sodium: 233mg

CABBAGE TURKEY SOUP

Servings: 1

Cooking Time: 40 min

- ½ cup shredded green cabbage
- ½ cup bulgur
- 2 dried bay leaves
- 2 tablespoons chopped fresh parsley
- 1 teaspoon chopped fresh sage
- 1 teaspoon chopped fresh thyme
- 1 celery stalk, chopped
- 1 carrot, sliced thin
- ½ sweet onion, chopped
- 1 teaspoon minced garlic
- 1 teaspoon olive oil
- ½ pound cooked ground turkey, 93% lean
- 4 cups water
- 1 cup chicken stock
- Pinch red pepper flakes
- Black pepper (ground), to taste

Directions:

1. Take a large saucepan or cooking pot and add the oil. Heat over medium heat.
2. Add turkey and stir-cook for 4-5 minutes until evenly brown.
3. Add onion and garlic and sauté for about 3 minutes to soften veggies.
4. Add water, chicken stock, cabbage, bulgur, celery, carrot, and bay leaves. Boil the mixture.
5. Over low heat, cover and simmer the mixture for about 30-35 minutes until bulgur is cooked well and tender.
6. Remove bay leaves. Add parsley, sage, thyme, and red pepper flakes; stir mixture and season with black pepper. Serve warm.

Per Serving:

Calories: 267; Total Fat: 10g; Saturated Fat: 2; Sodium: 738mg; Total Carbs: 16; Sugar: 8g; Protein: 28g; Fiber: 6g; Cholesterol 32mg

---

LIME LENTIL SOUP

Servings: 2

Cooking Time: 35 min

- 1 tsp olive oil
- 1 onion, chopped
- 6 garlic cloves, minced
- 1 tsp chili powder
- ½ tsp ground cinnamon
- Sea salt to taste

- 1 cup yellow lentils
- 1 cup canned diced tomatoes

- 1 celery stalk, chopped
- 10 oz chopped collard greens

Directions:

1. Heat oil in an iron pot over medium heat. Place onion and garlic and cook for 5 minutes. Stir in chili powder, celery, cinnamon, and salt. Pour in lentils, tomatoes and juices, and 2 cups of water. Bring to a boil, then set to low heat and cook for 15 minutes.
2. Stir in collard greens. Cook for an additional 5 minutes. Serve in bowls and enjoy!

Per Serving:

Calories: 320;Fat: 14g; Saturated Fat: 2g; Sodium: 1120mg; Total Carbs: 41g; Sugar: 4g; Protein: 14g; Fiber: 7g; cholesterol: 0mg

---

CHEESY SALMON & VEGETABLE SOUP

Servings: 2

Cooking Time: 20 min

- 1 cup low-sodium chicken stock
- 1 ½ cups warm water
- 1 large carrot, thinly sliced (1/2-inch thick slices)
- 1 large russet potato, cut into 1 1/2-inch thick pieces
- 1 cup button mushrooms, thinly sliced
- ¼ cup low-fat evaporated milk

- 1 tbsp. all-purpose flour
- ¼ cup strong cheddar cheese, grated
- ½ lb. wild salmon fillets, cut into 1 ½ -inch pieces
- 1/8 tsp. kosher salt
- ¼ tsp. white pepper
- 1 tbsp. fresh dill, chopped

Directions:

1. Whisk together the chicken stock, water, carrots, and potato in a large pot over medium-high heat. Bring the soup to a boil while stirring. Once the soup begins to boil, lower the heat to medium, and simmer for 10-15 minutes, or until the vegetables are tender. Stir at regular intervals to prevent burning. Add in the mushrooms.
2. Whisk together the evaporated milk and flour to form a lump-free paste in a glass bowl. Whisk the paste into the soup, and bring the soup back up to a boil while stirring. Return the soup to a moderate simmer and toss in the cheese until it is completely integrated into the soup.
3. With the heat on medium-low, stir in the salmon, and cook for 3-4 minutes, until the fish is entirely opaque and flaky. Stir in the salt and pepper after removing the pot from the heat.
4. Ladle the soup into bowls, and garnish with the fresh dill before serving hot.

Per Serving:

Calories: 398; Total Fat: 14g; Saturated Fat: 4g; Carbohydrates: 37g; Protein: 30g; Sodium: 647 mg; Fiber: 3g

MIXED VEGETABLES WITH TURMERIC

Servings: 4

Cooking Time: 60 min

- 2 ½ cups mixed legumes (lentils, cannellini, red beans, broad beans, etc.)
- 1 cup cherry tomatoes
- 2 carrots
- 2 celery stalks
- 3 tablespoons of extra virgin olive oil
- One small white onion
- Turmeric powder as needed
- Salt to taste

Directions:

1. To realize this recipe, it is suggested to use dried legumes. In this regard, it is advisable to place the legumes to soak overnight. At the moment of preparation, remove residual water and keep legumes aside.
2. Then, wash vegetables, remove scraps and chop them thoroughly; at this point, put everything in a large pot.
3. Add legumes and cover everything with water; then, cook over low heat for one hour; if necessary, add water from time to time, avoiding legumes to stick to the bottom.
4. At the end of cooking, remove any excess water and add salt, raw oil and turmeric; then mix carefully, portion and serve.

Per Serving:

Calories: 184; Total Fat: 12g; Saturated Fat: 2,8g; Sodium: 66mg; Total Carbs: 13g; Sugar: 6g; Protein: 2g

---

WHOLE WHEAT BARLEY WITH HERBS

Servings: 4

Cooking Time: 20 min

- 1 ½ cups whole barley
- 3 bunches of aromatic herbs (sage, basil and marjoram)
- 3 tablespoons of extra-virgin olive oil
- One small white onion
- Salt to taste
- Black pepper to taste

Directions:

1. First, it is preferable to soak the barley overnight before using it.
2. Wash and trim the aromatic herbs and the spring onion; then chop everything and keep aside.
3. Pour the barley into a medium-sized saucepan (made of aluminum or copper) and proceed to dry-roast it for one minute; then, add water from time to time, proceeding to cook the barley.
4. Meanwhile, blend the herbs with the spring onion and olive oil; add small amounts of salt and black pepper to the mixture.
5. Halfway through cooking, add herb mixture to barley and stir thoroughly; continue stirring and adding water until cooked through; portion and serve.

Per Serving:

Calories: 121; Total Fat: 4g; Saturated Fat: 0,5g; Total Carbs: 19g; Protein: 3g

---

WHOLE WHEAT LINGUINE WITH ARUGULA PESTO, TOASTED PINE NUTS AND WALNUTS

Servings: 4

Cooking Time: 10 min

- 10 oz. whole wheat linguine
- 2 bunches of arugula
- 3 tablespoons extra virgin olive oil
- 2 tablespoons pine nuts
- 2 tablespoons shelled walnuts
- Salt to taste.

Directions:

1. First, pour water into a medium-sized pot, filling it up to half of its capacity, then, bring the water to a boil; add a small amount of salt and pour in the linguine to be cooked.
2. In the meantime, proceed to thoroughly wash and clean the arugula, placing it immediately afterward, in a blender with olive oil and a small amount of salt; then, blend everything until a smooth mixture is obtained and set aside;
3. Next, toast the pine nuts in a preheated skillet over low heat, getting the proper browning; keep the pine nuts aside; with the help of a cutting board, chop the nuts coarsely;
4. After cooking is almost complete, drain the pasta and add the arugula pesto, toasted pine nuts and chopped nuts; then, whisk everything over low heat for half a minute; finally, portion and serve the pasta still hot.

Per Serving:

Calories: 434; Total Fat: 12g; Saturated Fat: 2,5g; Total Carbs: 32g; Sugar: 2g; Protein: 16g; Fiber: 3g, Sodium: 287mg; Cholesterol: 27mg

LENTILS & RICE

Servings: 4

Cooking Time: 40 min

- 6 cups water
- 1 tsp Himalayan pink salt, divided
- 1 cup wild rice
- 1 cup dried brown lentils, picked over
- 3 tbsp olive oil, more if needed

- 2 medium-sized yellow onions, thinly sliced
- ½ cup cilantro, finely chopped
- 6 spring onions, sliced, divided
- Ground black pepper

Directions:

1. In a large saucepan, bring the water and ¾ tsp of Himalayan pink salt to a boil over high heat. Add the wild rice, and cook for 10 minutes.
2. Add the picked over lentils and mix to combine. Put the lid on and simmer for about 25 minutes, or until rice and lentils are tender. Remove from the heat, and drain any remaining liquid. Allow resting for 10 minutes.
3. Heat the olive oil in a large, heavy-bottom pan over high heat. Line a plate with paper towels.
4. Add the sliced onions, and cook for 20 minutes, or until well browned. Transfer the onions to the plate to drain. Sprinkle with the remaining ¼ tsp Himalayan pink salt.
5. Mix half the fried onions, the chopped cilantro, and sliced spring onion into the lentils and rice mixture.
6. Divide the lentils and rice mixture, and garnish each serving with fried onion and sliced spring onions. Season with ground black pepper to taste.

Per Serving:

Calories: 333; Total Fat: 10g; Saturated Fat: 7g; Sodium: 399mg; Total Carbs: 50g; Fiber: 6g; Protein:11g

ROASTED CHICKPEAS

Servings: 4

Cooking Time: 20 min

- 14 oz. (1 can) chickpeas, rinsed and drained
- 1/2 tsp smoked paprika

- 1/2 tsp cinnamon
- 1 tbsp apple cider vinegar

- 1/2 tsp maple syrup
- 1/2 tsp dried basil leaves
- 1/2 tsp ground cumin
- A pinch of sea salt

Directions:

1. Preheat the oven to 425 F and line a baking sheet with baking paper.
2. Mix chickpeas, paprika, vinegar, cumin, basil, cinnamon, syrup, and salt in a large bowl. Stir to combine.
3. Spread evenly on the baking sheet and bake for 20 minutes, or until the marinade is soaked up. Serve warm.

Per Serving:

Calories: 163; Total Fat: 3g; Saturated Fat: 0,3; Total Carbs: 24,9g; Sugar: 4,7g; Protein: 7,5g; Fiber: 6,9g, Sodium: 155mg; Cholesterol: 0mg

---

GINGER BROWN RICE

Servings: 3

Cooking Time: 40 min

- 1 cup brown rice, rinsed
- 1-inch grated ginger
- ½ of serrano pepper, chopped
- 1 green onion, chopped
- 2 cups of water

Directions:

1. Take a medium pot, place it over medium-high heat, and pour in water.
2. Add rice, green onion, serrano pepper, and ginger, bring to a boil, switch heat to medium and then simmer for 30 minutes.
3. Divide rice among three bowls and then serve.

Per Serving:

Calories: 184; Total Fat: 12g; Saturated Fat: 2,8g; Sodium: 66mg; Total Carbs: 13g; Sugar: 6g; Protein: 2g

---

KALE TACOS

Servings: 8 tacos

- 1 cup cooked black beans
- 1 cup chopped kale
- ½ of a medium avocado, sliced
- 1 cup chopped white onion
- 1 cup chopped tomatoes
- 2 tablespoons chopped cilantro

- ½ teaspoon minced garlic
- 2/3 teaspoon salt
- ½ of a lemon
- 1 tablespoon water
- 8 small tacos

Directions:

1. Place beans in a medium bowl, add salt, cumin powder, and then mash with a fork until beans have broken.
2. Take a medium skillet pan, place it over medium heat, add water, add kale and garlic, then cook for 4 minutes or until softened, set aside until required.
3. Heat the tacos until thoroughly warmed, fold each taco in half, spread 1 tablespoon of bean mixture on one-half side of taco, and then top with tomatoes, onion, avocado, kale, and cilantro.
4. Drizzle with lemon juice, fold, and then serve.

Per Serving:

Calories: 109.9 Cal; Fat: 2.9 g; Protein: 4.9 g; Carbs: 17 g; Fiber: 5 g;

ROASTED BRUSSEL SPROUTS

Servings: 4

Cooking Time: 30 min

- 3 cups Brussel sprouts
- ½ cup dried cranberries
- 1 ½ teaspoon salt

- 1 teaspoon ground black pepper
- 2 tablespoons olive oil

Directions:

1. Switch on the oven, then set it to 375 degrees F and let it preheat.
2. Meanwhile, cut each Brussel sprout in half and place them in a large bowl.
3. Add salt and black pepper, drizzle with oil, toss until coated, and spread on a baking sheet.
4. Add cranberries to it, and then roast the Brussel sprouts for 30 minutes until cooked.
5. Serve straight away.

Per Serving:

Calories: 135 Cal; Fat: 9.8 g; Protein: 3.9 g; Carbs: 11 g; Fiber: 4 g;

VEGETABLE WITH BROWN RICE

Servings: 4

Cooking Time: 55 min

- 16-ounce extra-firm tofu, pressed, drained
- 1 cup broccoli florets
- 1 cup brown rice, rinsed
- 1 small white onion, peeled, diced
- 1 ½ tablespoon minced garlic
- 1 medium red bell pepper, cored, diced
- 1 tablespoon olive oil
- 2 cups of water

Directions:

1. Take a medium pot, place it over medium-high heat, add rice, pour in the water, and then bring to a boil.
2. Then switch heat to medium-low level, cover the pot with the lid and then cook the rice for 40 minutes, set aside until required.
3. Place oil in a large skillet pan, place it over medium-high heat and let it heat.
4. Cut tofu into ½-inch cubes, add into the pan along with broccoli, onion, bell pepper, and garlic, and then cook for 5 minutes until vegetables become tender.
5. Add rice into the pan, toss until mixed, and then cook for 5 minutes until hot.
6. Serve straight away.

Per Serving:

Calories: 279.4 Cal; Fat: 8 g; Protein: 10.5 g; Carbs: 45.8 g; Fiber: 5 g;

CHORIZO MEAT

Servings: 2

Cooking Time: 10 min

- 15-ounce cooked chickpeas
- 2 cups California walnuts
- 2 teaspoons salt
- 2 ½ teaspoons dried oregano
- 2 teaspoons nutritional yeast
- 2 teaspoons ground chipotle
- 2 teaspoons ground coriander
- 2 tablespoons ground cumin

- ½ tablespoon white vinegar
- ¼ cup olive oil

Directions:

1. Place all the ingredients in a blender or a food processor and then pulse for 1 to 2 minutes until the mixture resemble rice.
2. Spoon the mixture into a medium skillet pan, place it over medium-low heat and then cook for 5 to 7 minutes until thoroughly warmed.
3. Serve straight away.

Per Serving:

Calories: 150 Cal; Fat: 13 g; Protein: 4 g; Carbs: 7 g; Fiber: 3 g;

LENTIL VEGETABLE CURRY

Servings: 4

Cooking Time: 25 min

- 2 cups cooked brown rice
- 1 ½ cup cooked brown lentils
- 2 cups of frozen mixed vegetables
- 1 ½ cups diced potatoes
- ½ cup diced white onion
- 1 cup diced red bell peppers

- 2 teaspoons minced garlic
- 2 dried red peppers, minced
- 3 tablespoons red curry paste
- 1 tablespoon olive oil
- 2 cups coconut milk, unsweetened

Directions:

1. Take a heatproof bowl, add diced potatoes, and then microwave for 1 minute or until softened.
2. Place oil in a large pot, place it over medium-high heat, and then heat it hot.
3. Add onion, potatoes, and bell pepper, stir in garlic, red pepper, and curry paste and then cook for 10 minutes.
4. Pour in the milk, continue cooking the curry for 10 minutes until vegetables turn tender, and stir in lentils.
5. Cook the curry for 3 minutes until thoroughly hot and then serve.

Per Serving:

Calories: 210 Cal; Fat: 3.2 g; Protein: 12.2 g; Carbs: 35.1 g; Fiber: 13.7 g;

BLACK BEAN STEW

Servings: 6

Cooking Time: 15 min

- 2 green onions, chopped
- 3 celery, chopped
- ½ of serrano pepper, chopped
- 1 teaspoon grated ginger
- 1 tablespoon lemon zest
- 2 cups cooked black beans
- 1 tablespoon olive oil

Directions:

1. Take a large skillet pan, place it over medium-high heat, add oil and let it heat.
2. Add black beans, pour in the broth, and then bring it to a boil.
3. Switch heat to medium level, add onions, celery, ginger, and serrano pepper, stir until mixed, and cook for 3 to 5 minutes until vegetables are tender-crisp.
4. Serve the stew with cooked brown rice.

Per Serving:

Calories: 253 Cal; Fat: 5 g; Protein: 32 g; Carbs: 107 g; Fiber: 36 g;

SWEET POTATO AND CORN CHOWDER

Servings: 4

Cooking Time: 20 min

- 4 cups canned corn
- ½ of red onion, peeled, cut into ½-inch cubes
- 1 medium sweet potato, peeled, cut into ½-inch cubes
- 1 medium red bell pepper, cored, cut into ½-inch cubes
- 2 tablespoons minced garlic
- ½ teaspoon smoked paprika
- 2 teaspoons avocado oil
- 1 tablespoon lemon juice
- 4 cups vegetable broth
- 2 tablespoons chopped basil

Directions:

1. Take a large pot, place it over medium heat, add oil, and heat it until hot.
2. Add onion, cook for 2 minutes, stir in garlic and then continue cooking for 1 minute until fragrant.

3. Add sweet potato and bell pepper pieces, cook for 2 minutes, add corn, stir in paprika, and pour in vegetable stock.
4. Simmer the vegetables for 15 minutes until tender. Then remove the pot from heat and puree the mixture by using an immersion blender until smooth.
5. Add salt, black pepper, lemon juice, and basil into the chowder, stir until mixed, and then ladle into four bowls.
6. Serve straight away.

Per Serving:

Calories: 220 Cal; Fat: 3.8 g; Protein: 6.5 g; Carbs: 46.2 g; Fiber: 6.3 g;

CHICKEN WITH BLACK OLIVES, CAPERS AND RICE OIL

Servings: 4

Cooking Time: 35 min

- 17 oz. of chicken breast
- 4 tablespoons pitted black olives
- 3 tablespoons capers
- 3 tablespoons rice oil

- Flour to taste
- Salt to taste
- Black pepper to taste

Directions:

1. For a better yield in seasoning, it is preferable to chop the olives into smaller pieces; then, wash the capers under running water to remove the salt from them.
2. At this point, flour the chicken breast lightly, then place it in a baking pan (cover the bottom of the pan with a sheet of baking paper).
3. Then, cover the chicken breast with the olives and capers, adding a little salt and pepper seasoning; bake at 180°C for 15 minutes.
4. When cooked, season the chicken by distributing the indicated amount of rice oil; portion and serve

Per Serving:

Calories: 184; Total Fat: 12g; Saturated Fat: 2,8g; Sodium: 166mg; Total Carbs: 3g; Sugar: 2g; Protein: 12g

---

BASIL PESTO CHICKEN

Servings: 4

Cooking Time: 15 min

- 8 oz uncooked rotini pasta
- 1 lb. asparagus, woody ends removed, cut into bite-size pieces
- 1 tbsp coconut oil
- 2 medium Roma tomatoes, chopped

- ½ cup basil pesto
- 12 oz boneless, cut into bite-size cubes, skinless chicken breasts
- ¼ cup Parmesan cheese, grated

Directions:

1. Follow the package directions for cooking the rotini pasta or al dente. Scoop out ½ cup of the cooking water, and keep to one side. Add the asparagus pieces to the pasta when it reaches the remaining 4 minutes. Allow boiling.
2. Heat the coconut oil over medium-high heat in a large, heavy-bottom pan. Fry the cubed chicken breasts for 5 to 10 minutes or until cooked through. Stir in the chopped tomatoes, and remove the pan from the heat.
3. Drain the pasta and asparagus in a colander, and return them to the stockpot.
4. Toss the pasta and asparagus with the basil pesto and ¼ cup of the reserved cooking water. Add the cooked chicken mixture and more cooking water if needed.
5. Top with the grated Parmesan cheese, and serve hot.

Per Serving:

Calories: 485; Total Fat: 17g; Saturated Fat: 4g; Cholesterol: 68mg; Sodium: 201mg; Total Carbs: 50g; Fiber: 5g; Protein: 33g

---

OLIVE TURKEY PATTIES

Servings: 4

Cooking Time: 30 min

- Aluminum foil
- 1 lb. lean ground turkey
- ½ cup rolled oats
- ¼ cup sliced black olives, chopped
- ¼ cup white onion, finely chopped
- ¼ cup parsley, finely chopped

- 1 tbsp garlic, minced
- 6 whole-wheat hamburger buns
- 1 ripe avocado, peeled, pitted, and sliced
- 6 iceberg lettuce leaves
- 6 beefsteak tomato slices

Directions:

1. Preheat the broiler and set a baking sheet about 3 inches from the heat source. Line a baking sheet with aluminum foil.
2. In a large mixing bowl, add the ground turkey, rolled oats, chopped black olives, chopped onion, chopped parsley, and minced garlic. Mix well until combined. Shape into 6 equal patties.
3. Place the turkey patties on the baking sheet, and broil for 3 to 4 minutes on each side, or until the juices run clear.
4. Meanwhile, place the whole-wheat buns, sliced avocado, iceberg lettuce, and tomato slices on a serving platter. Allow diners to assemble their burgers.

Per Serving:

Calories: 366; Total Fat: 15g; Saturated Fat: 3g; Cholesterol: 52mg; Sodium: 353mg; Total Carbs: 35g; Fiber: 6g; Protein: 24g

GARLIC TURKEY SKEWERS

Servings: 4

Cooking Time: 15 min

- 1 lb. boneless, skinless turkey breasts, cut into cubes
- 1 lemon, juiced
- 2 tbsp avocado oil
- 2 tbsp garlic, crushed
- 1 tsp dried thyme
- 1 tsp dried oregano
- ½ tsp fine sea salt
- ¼ tsp ground black pepper

Directions:

1. Combine the turkey cubes, lemon juice, avocado oil, crushed garlic, dried thyme, dried oregano, fine sea salt, and ground black pepper in a large mixing bowl. Mix until well coated, and allow to rest for 30 minutes.
2. Spear the turkey cubes onto 8 skewers.
3. Over medium-high heat, heat a nonstick frying pan.
4. Place the skewers in the pan, and cook for 5 to 7 minutes. Flip and cook for 5 to 8 minutes, or until fully cooked and browned. Remove from the heat, and serve.

Per Serving:

Calories: 205; Total Fat: 10g; Saturated Fat: 2g; Sodium: 343mg; Total Carbs: 2g; Fiber: 0g; Protein: 26g

ALMOND BUTTER CHICKEN

Servings: 2

Cooking Time: 5 min

- 2 tsp olive oil
- 1 tbsp garlic, crushed, divided
- ½ cup brown onion, finely chopped
- 8 oz lean ground chicken
- 1 tsp ginger, grated
- 3 tbsp unsalted almond butter
- 4 tbsp water
- 6 large iceberg lettuce leaves

Directions:

1. Heat the olive oil in an iron pan over medium heat. Add half of the crushed garlic and the chopped onion, and cook until translucent for 1 to 2 minutes.
2. Add the ground chicken, break it up with a fork, and cook for 5 minutes, until golden and cooked through.
3. Add together the grated ginger, remaining crushed garlic, almond butter, and water in a glass bowl, and mix to combine. Add the almond butter mixture to the chicken mixture, and cook for 1 minute until the flavors have combined.
4. Divide the chicken mixture into the iceberg lettuce cups, and serve.

Per Serving:

Calories: 414; Total Fat: 21g; Saturated Fat: 4g; Cholesterol: 90mg; Sodium: 211mg; Total Carbs: 17g; Net Carbs: 7g; Fiber: 4g; Protein: 32g

BALSAMIC BERRY CHICKEN

Servings: 2

Cooking Time: 30 min

- Aluminum foil
- ½ cup blueberries
- 2 tbsp pine nuts
- ¼ cup basil, finely chopped
- 2 tbsp balsamic vinegar
- ¼ tsp ground black pepper
- 2 (4 oz) chicken breasts, butterflied

Directions:

1. Heat the oven to 375F, gas mark 5. Line a medium-sized baking dish with aluminum foil.
2. Add together the blueberries, pine nuts, chopped basil, balsamic vinegar, and ground black pepper in a medium-sized mixing bowl. Mix until well combined.
3. Place the chicken pieces in the pan, and pour the blueberry mixture on top.
4. Bake for 20 to 30 minutes, or until the juices are caramelized, and the inside of the chicken is fully cooked.
5. Serve warm with a side dish of your choice.

Tip: to butterfly a chicken breast, cut the breast halfway through, horizontally.

Substitution tip: swap the blueberries for any berry of your choice.

Per Serving:

Calories: 212; Total Fat: 7g; Saturated Fat: 1g; Cholesterol: 80mg; Sodium: 58mg; Total Carbs: 11g; Net Carbs: 7g; Fiber: 2g; Protein: 27g

Broccoli Chicken Rice

Servings: 4

Cooking Time: 20 min

- 1 lb. boneless, skinless chicken breasts, halved lengthwise
- ½ tsp Italian seasoning
- ½ tsp sea salt
- ¼ tsp ground black pepper
- 2 tbsp avocado oil, divided
- 4 cups broccoli rice
- 1 (15 oz) can artichoke hearts, drained
- ¼ cup capers

Directions:

1. Season the chicken with Italian seasoning, sea salt, and ground black pepper.
2. Warm 1 tbsp of avocado oil in a large, heavy-bottom pan over medium-high heat.
3. Add the seasoned chicken breasts and cook for 3 to 5 minutes or browned.
4. Flip and cook for 4 to 6 mins, or until fully cooked. Transfer onto a cutting board and thinly slice the chicken.
5. Heat the last 1 tbsp avocado oil in the same pan. Add the broccoli rice, and cook for 5 to 8 minutes, frequently stirring, until tender.
6. Add the artichoke hearts and capers, and mix until fully incorporated. Remove from the heat.
7. Serve the broccoli rice and vegetables, and top with the sliced chicken breasts.

Ingredient tip: Broccoli rice is broccoli florets that is chopped into the size of rice grains.

Per Serving:

Calories: 270; Total Fat: 11g; Saturated Fat: 2g; Sodium: 481mg; Total Carbs: 14g; Fiber: 6g; Protein: 30g

Chicken Meatballs

Servings: 4

Cooking Time: 15 min

- Aluminum foil
- 1 lb. lean ground chicken
- 1 cup courgettes, shredded
- ½ cup red onion, finely diced
- 3 tbsp black olives, minced
- 1 tbsp Mediterranean Seasoning Rub Blend

- 1 cup grape tomatoes

Directions:

1. Heat the oven to broil, and set an oven rack 6 inches from the broiler. Line a baking sheet with aluminum foil.
2. In a wide-sized mixing bowl, combine the ground chicken, shredded courgettes, diced onion, minced black olives, and Mediterranean seasoning blend. Allow marinating for at 10 minutes.
3. Mold each tbsp of the chicken mixture into a meatball to make 8 total, and place them on the baking sheet with the grape tomatoes.
4. Broil for 6 to 12 minutes, until golden brown and fully cooked. The tomatoes should be blistered.
5. Serve with your choice of side.

Per Serving:

Calories: 160; Total Fat: 5g; Saturated Fat: 1g; Cholesterol: 90mg; Sodium: 107mg; Total Carbs: 6g; Net Carbs: 3g; Fiber: 2g; Protein: 24g

---

LEMON-SIMMERED CHICKEN & ARTICHOKES

Servings: 4

Cooking Time: 10-15 min

- 4 boneless chicken breast halves, skins removed
- 1/4 tsp. Himalayan salt
- 1/4 tsp. freshly ground black pepper
- 2 tsp. avocado oil
- 1 tbsp. lemon juice
- 2 tsp. dried crushed oregano
- ¼ cup Kalamata olives pitted and halved
- 2/3 cup reduced-sodium chicken stock
- 14 oz. canned, water-packed, quartered artichoke hearts

Directions:

1. Toss the chicken breasts with salt and pepper before cooking. In a large frying pan, heat the oil over medium-high heat. Brown the chicken on all sides once the oil is nice and hot – about 2-4 minutes per side.
2. When the chicken is nicely browned, stir in the lemon juice, oregano, olives, chicken stock, and artichoke hearts. Lower the heat to low and cover the pan when the stock begins to boil. Simmer for 4-5 minutes, or until the chicken is thoroughly cooked. Serve hot.

Per Serving:

Calories: 225; Total Fat: 9g; Saturated Fat: 1g; Carbohydrates: 9g; Protein: 26g; Sodium: 864g; Fiber: 0g

GROUND TURKEY MINCE

Servings: 4

Cooking Time: 10-15 min

- 2 tbsp. avocado oil
- 1 lb. lean ground turkey
- 2 tsp. crushed garlic
- 1 red bell pepper, seeded and diced
- 1 small shallot, chopped
- 1/2 tsp. ground cumin
- 1/2 tsp. ground cinnamon

- Freshly ground black pepper
- 1/4 tsp. kosher salt
- 2 tbsp. hummus
- 1/4 cup chicken bone broth
- 1 lemon, finely zested
- 1 tbsp. lemon juice
- Fresh parsley, chopped, for garnish

Directions:

1. Heat 1 tbsp of the oil in a large frying pan over medium-high heat. When the oil is nice and hot, add the ground turkey, and fry for about 5 minutes in a single layer, without stirring. After 5 minutes, flip the meat with a spatula, and stir to separate all the bits. Scrape into a bowl, and set aside.
2. Return the pan to medium-low heat, and add the remaining oil. Fry the garlic, bell peppers, and shallots in the heated oil for about 5 minutes or until the veggies are soft. Before returning the ground turkey to the pan, stir in the cumin and cinnamon for about 30 seconds, a generous teaspoon of pepper, salt, hummus, chicken broth, lemon zest and lemon juice. Stir for 5 minutes.
3. Serve the ground turkey on wraps of your choice, garnished with the fresh parsley.

Per Serving:

Calories: 280; Total Fat: 17g; Carbohydrates: 10g; Protein: 23g; Sodium: 251mg; Fiber: 2g

VEGETABLE & HERB CHICKEN CACCIATORE

Servings: 6-8

Cooking Time: 1 hour 10 min

- 1 cup boiling water
- 1/2 oz. dried porcini mushrooms
- 2 tbsp. avocado oil

- 12 boneless chicken thighs, skins removed and fat trimmed

- 1 large fennel bulb, cored, halved, and thinly sliced
- 1 large shallot, halved and thinly sliced
- 1 green bell pepper, seeded, and chopped into rings
- 1 tsp. fresh thyme leaves, chopped
- 2 tsp. finely grated orange zest
- 1 tbsp. fresh rosemary, chopped
- 3 tsp. crushed garlic
- 3 tbsp. balsamic vinegar
- 1 tsp. kosher salt
- 2 tbsp. tomato paste
- 3/4 cup dry white wine

Directions:

1. Set the oven to preheat to 350F, with the wire rack in the center of the oven.
2. Place the boiling water and mushrooms in a large bowl and soak on the counter for 20 minutes.
3. Meanwhile, heat the olive oil in a wide frying saucepan over medium heat before adding the chicken thighs and browning on all sides. If required, cook the chicken in batches to avoid overloading the saucepan. Transfer the cooked thighs to a large casserole dish.
4. Lower the heat, add the fennel, shallots, and bell pepper to the same pan, frying for 7 minutes, or until the vegetables are fork-tender. Add the thyme, zest, rosemary, and garlic. Fry for 30 seconds before adding the vinegar and frying for an additional 1 minute.
5. Finely chop the soaked mushrooms before adding them to the pan, along with the soaking water, salt, tomato paste, and wine.
6. Once the sauce begins to boil, carefully pour the contents of the pan over the thighs in the casserole dish. Cover the plate with foil, and bake for 45 minutes.
7. Allow the cooked thighs to stand on the counter for 5-10 minutes before serving hot.

Per Serving:

Calories: 468; Total Fat: 19g; Saturated Fat: 5g; Carbohydrates: 9g; Protein: 58g; Sodium: 527mg; Fiber: 3g

Beef, Pork and Lamb

SLOW ROASTED BEEF

Servings: 6

Cooking Time: 1 hour 15 min

- 1 tbsp olive oil
- 1 medium yellow onion, sliced
- 1 tbsp garlic, minced
- 1½ lb. beef roast, cut into pieces

- 1 (28 oz) can whole tomatoes with their juices
- ¼ tsp sea salt
- ½ tsp ground black pepper
- ¼ cup cilantro, finely chopped

Directions:

1. Heat the oven to 350°F, gas mark 4.
2. Heat the olive oil over high heat in a cast iron or oven-safe pot.
3. Add the sliced onion and cook for 3 to 5 minutes or softened.
4. Add the minced garlic, and cook for 30 seconds until fragrant.
5. Add the beef pieces, and fry for 5 to 6 minutes, until browned on all sides.
6. Add the whole tomatoes with their juices, sea salt, and ground black pepper. Allow to boil, and turn off the heat.
7. Place the saucepan in the oven and cover it with a lid. Cook for 1 hour, or until the meat is tender, stirring occasionally, and scraping the bottom. Remove from the oven, and let it chill for 10 minutes.
8. Use a spoon to skim any fat from the top of the mixture.
9. Serve the roast with your choice of vegetables, and sprinkle with chopped cilantro.

Per Serving:

Calories: 202; Total Fat: 9g; Saturated Fat: 2g; Sodium: 460mg; Total Carbs: 7g; Fiber: 3g; Protein: 25g

---

LENTIL BEEF BOLOGNESE

Servings: 6

Cooking Time: 30 min

- 1 lb. lean ground beef
- ½ tsp fine sea salt, divided
- Ground black pepper

- 1 small red onion, chopped
- 1 tbsp garlic, minced
- ½ cup uncooked red lentils, rinsed

- 1 (28 oz) can whole, no-salt-added tomatoes with their juices
- 1 lb. white mushrooms, sliced
- ⅔ cup water
- 2 tbsp tomato paste
- 1 tbsp Italian seasoning

Directions:

1. Heat a large iron pan over high heat. Once hot, add the ground beef, breaking it up with a fork, and season with ¼ tsp salt and some ground black pepper. Cook for 4 minutes, or until browned.
2. Cook, turning periodically, for 5 to 7 minutes, until the beef is no longer pink, adding the chopped onion and minced garlic.
3. Add the red lentils, whole tomatoes with their juice, sliced mushrooms, water, tomato paste, and Italian seasoning. Reduce the heat to low, simmer and stirring occasionally, for 15 minutes, or until the lentils are mushy. Season with salt and pepper to taste.
4. Serve over zucchini noodles or spaghetti squash.

Per Serving:

Calories: 212; Total Fat: 4g; Saturated Fat: 2g; Cholesterol: 48mg; Sodium: 266mg; Total Carbs: 21g; Fiber: 5g; Protein: 24g

---

PORK MEDALLIONS

Servings: 4

Cooking Time: 30 min

- 1 (1 lb.) boneless pork tenderloin roast, sliced into thick medallions
- ¼ tsp sea salt
- Ground black pepper
- 1 tbsp avocado oil
- 1 large brown onion, cut into wedges
- 1 cup reduced-sodium chicken stock
- 1 lb. baby carrots
- 2 tbsp organic honey
- ¼ tsp ground cinnamon
- ¼ tsp ground cumin
- ¼ tsp ground turmeric
- 1 cup uncooked couscous
- 1 tsp lime juice

Directions:

1. Season the pork medallions with sea salt and ground black pepper.
2. In a large, heavy-bottomed skillet, heat the avocado oil until hot. Cook the pork for 3 minutes per side until browned on both sides. Transfer to a plate and cover.

3. Reduce the heat to medium-low and cook the onion wedges for 3 to 4 minutes, or until they are softened. Heat the chicken stock, baby carrots, organic honey, ground cinnamon, ground cumin, and ground turmeric over high heat. Mix to combine.
4. When the stock is boiling, turn the heat down to low, and cook for 7 to 8 minutes until the carrots are tender.
5. Prepare the couscous according to package directions.
6. Replace the pork medallions to the pan with the lime juice and cook until well cooked. Serve the pork and vegetables over the couscous.

Per Serving:

Calories: 426; Total Fat: 7g; Saturated Fat: 1g; Cholesterol: 83mg; Sodium: 347mg; Total Carbs: 55g; Fiber: 6g; Protein: 35g

---

LAMB GOULASH

Servings: 4

Cooking Time: 50 min

- 2 tbsp olive oil
- 1 lb. boneless lamb shoulder, diced
- 1 large brown onion, finely chopped
- 2 large carrots, peeled and chopped
- 15 oz can garbanzo beans, drained and rinsed

- 1 tsp paprika
- 1 tsp ground coriander
- ½ tsp ground ginger
- 4 cups water
- Fine sea salt
- Ground black pepper

Directions:

1. In a large iron saucepan, heat the olive oil over high heat.
2. Add the diced lamb and brown for 3 to 5 minutes per side. Leave the juices in the pot, and transfer the lamb onto a plate.
3. Add the chopped onion and chopped carrots to the pot, and cook for 3 to 5 minutes, or until softened.
4. Add the garbanzo beans, paprika, ground coriander and ground ginger, and mix to combine.
5. Transfer the lamb back into the pot, along with the juices collected on the plate. Add the water, and allow to boil.
6. Reduce the heat to low, cover, and simmer for 30 to 40 minutes, or until the lamb is tender. Remove from the heat, and season with sea salt and ground black pepper to taste. Serve immediately.

Per Serving:

Calories: 389; Total Fat: 21g; Saturated Fat: 7g; Sodium: 501mg; Total Carbs: 20g; Fiber: 5g; Protein: 26g

PAN FRIED SIRLOIN

Servings: 4

Cooking Time: 25 min

- 1 cup uncooked quinoa
- 1 tbsp olive oil
- 12 oz sirloin beef, trimmed and thinly sliced
- ½ brown onion, finely chopped
- 1 medium green bell pepper, seeded and chopped
- 1 cup no-salt-added kidney beans, rinsed and drained
- ⅔ cup reduced-sodium chicken stock
- 1 tbsp Salt-Free Southwest Seasoning Mix, plus more if needed
- 1 ripe avocado, peeled, pitted, and diced
- ½ cup fresh tomato salsa

Directions:

1. Cook the 1 cup quinoa according to the package instructions.
2. Heat the olive oil in a heavy bottom pan over medium-high heat. Once hot, cook the beef slices for 3 to 4 minutes until cooked through. Transfer to a plate.
3. Fry the chopped onion and chopped green bell pepper for 4 to 5 minutes, until soft. Turn the heat down to medium.
4. Add the drained kidney beans, chicken stock, and Southwest seasoning. Cover, and cook for 5 minutes.
5. Add the cooked quinoa, and return the beef slices to the pan. Adjust the seasoning to taste, if desired, and warm through. Garnish with diced avocado and fresh tomato salsa.

Per Serving:

Calories: 440; Total Fat: 22g; Saturated Fat: 5g; Cholesterol: 59mg; Sodium: 158mg; Total Carbs: 36g; Fiber: 9g; Protein: 26g

---

PARMESAN PORK CHOPS

Servings: 4

Cooking Time: 25 min

- 2 tbsp avocado oil
- 4 thick pork chops, fat trimmed
- ½ red onion, chopped
- 1½ cups couscous
- 2½ cups water
- ½ cup sun-dried tomatoes, chopped

- 3 cups kale, finely chopped
- ¼ cup parmesan cheese, grated

Directions:

1. Warm the avocado oil in an iron pot over high heat.
2. Add the pork chops, and fry for 1½ minutes on each side, until browned. Transfer to a plate.
3. Reduce the heat to medium. Cook for 6 minutes or until the onion has softened.
4. Add the couscous, and cook for 1 to 2 minutes, until browned.
5. Put in the water and scrape the bottom of the pan to deglaze it.
6. Add the chopped sun-dried tomatoes, and allow to simmer for 5 minutes.
7. Add the pork chunks back to the pot, cover, and turn the heat down to low. Cook for 6 to 8 minutes, or until the chops are fully cooked and the couscous is tender.
8. Remove the iron pot from the heat and add the grated parmesan and chopped greens, stirring until the kale is wilted. Serve warm.

Tip: if the couscous starts to dry out, add 2 tbsp of water at a time to keep it moist.

Per Serving:

Calories: 484; Total Fat: 18g; Saturated Fat: 4g; Sodium: 103mg; Total Carbs: 48g; Fiber: 4g; Protein: 32g

---

STRIP STEAK QUINOA

Servings: 4

Cooking Time: 30 min

For the quinoa:

- 1 cup uncooked quinoa
- 12 oz strip steak, any fat trimmed
- ⅛ tsp fine sea salt
- Ground black pepper
- 1 tbsp olive oil
- 1 large iceberg lettuce head, finely chopped
- 2 spring onions, finely chopped
- ⅓ cup pine nuts

For the dressing:

- ¼ cup olive oil
- 3 tbsp apple cider vinegar
- 2 tbsp reduced-sodium tamari
- 2 tbsp organic honey

Directions:

For the quinoa:

1. Follow the package directions for cooking the quinoa. While it's cooking, place a medium-sized mixing bowl in the freezer. Once the quinoa is done cooking, take the mixing bowl out, and transfer the cooked quinoa to the bowl. Allow cooling for a few minutes.
2. Pat the strip steak dry with a paper towel, and season with fine sea salt and ground black pepper.
3. In a wide pan, warm the olive oil over high heat. When hot, add the strip steak and brown for 5 to 6 minutes on each side until done to your liking. Place the strip steak on a cutting board, and allow to rest for 5 minutes, then cut it into thin slices.

For the dressing:

1. In a large mixing bowl, combine the olive oil, apple cider vinegar, tamari, and organic honey, and whisk to incorporate.
2. Add the chopped iceberg lettuce, chopped spring onion, and cooled quinoa. Toss well with the dressing.
3. Serve dishes with strip steak pieces and pine nuts on top.

Per Serving:

Calories: 526; Total Fat: 29g; Saturated Fat: 5g; Cholesterol: 58mg; Sodium: 500mg; Total Carbs: 40g; Fiber: 5g; Protein: 30g

---

SPICY LIME PORK TENDERLOINS

Servings: 4

Cooking Time: 7 hours 15 min

- 2 lb pork tenderloins
- 1 cup chicken broth
- ¼ cup lime juice
- 3 tsp chili powder

- 2 tsp garlic powder
- 1 tsp ginger powder
- ½ tsp sea salt

Directions:

1. Combine chili powder, garlic powder, ginger powder, and salt in a bowl. Rub the spice mixture all over the pork and place it in the slow cooker. Pour in the broth and lime juice around the pork. Cover with the lid and cook for 7 hours on "Low".
2. Remove the pork from the slow cooker and let rest for 5 minutes. Slice the pork against the grain into medallions before serving.

Per Serving:

Calories: 182; Fat: 9g; Saturated Fat: 2g; Protein: 24g; Total Carbs: 1g; Sodium: 305mg; Cholesterol 74mg

DELIGHTFUL STUFFED LAMB WITH PEPPERS

Servings: 6

Cooking Time: 60 min

- 1 onion, finely diced
- 2 tablespoons water, plus additional for cooking
- 1½ pounds lamb, ground
- 1 cup grated zucchini

- ¼ cup fresh basil, minced
- 1 teaspoon salt
- 6 bell peppers, any color, seeded, ribbed, tops removed and reserved

Directions:

1. Preheat the oven to 350°F. Sauté the onion in the water in a large pan set over medium heat for 5 minutes, or until soft.
2. Add the ground lamb and zucchini. Cook for 10 minutes by breaking up the meat with a spoon.
3. Stir in the basil and salt. Remove from the heat.
4. Fill a casserole dish with 1½ inches of water.
5. Stuff each pepper with an equal amount of the lamb mixture and place them into the dish. Cap each pepper with its reserved top.
6. Place the dish in the preheated oven and bake for 45 to 50 minutes.

Per Serving:

Calories: 182; Fat: 27g; Saturated Fat: 12g; Protein: 22g; Total Carbs: 12g; Sodium: 681mg; Cholesterol 83mg

---

CHOPPED LAMBS WITH ROSEMARY

Servings: 4-6

Cooking Time: 7 to 8 hours

- 1 medium onion, sliced
- 2 teaspoons garlic powder
- 2 teaspoons rosemary, dried
- 1 teaspoon sea salt

- ½ teaspoon thyme leaves, dried
- Freshly ground black pepper
- 8 bone-in lamb chops, 3 pounds
- 2 tablespoons balsamic vinegar

Directions:

1. The onion slices should be used to line the bottom of the slow cooker.
2. Stir together the garlic powder, rosemary, salt, thyme, and pepper in a small bowl. Rub the chops evenly with the spice mixture and place gently in the slow cooker.
3. Drizzle the vinegar over the top.
4. Cover the cooker and set to low. Cook for 7 to 8 hours and serve.

Per Serving:

Calories: 251; Fat: 14,6g; Saturated Fat: 3,8g; Protein: 27,3g; Total Carbs: 1,3g; Sodium: 166mg; Cholesterol 85mg

Seafood

BAKED MACKEREL WITH ARTICHOKES AND ALMONDS

Servings: 4

Cooking Time: 30 min

- 21 oz. mackerel fillets
- 4 artichokes
- 2 tablespoons shelled almonds
- 3 tablespoons extra-virgin olive oil
- Lemon juice
- Salt to taste

Directions:

1. To begin, line a large baking pan with baking paper and preheat the oven to 350 degrees Fahrenheit.
2. In the meantime, you can proceed to peel the artichokes, removing the outer leaves and the terminal part of the stems; then, cut the artichokes into slices, put them in a bowl and cover them with lemon juice; moreover, chop the almonds obtaining some coarse fragments;
3. At this point, place the artichoke slices in the baking pan and cook for 15 minutes;
4. At the end of this cooking time, place the mackerel fillets on top of the artichokes, season with a small amount of salt and cover the surface with almond granules; then leave to cook for a further 15 minutes;
5. When cooked, dress the fillets with raw extra-virgin olive oil; portion and serve.

Per Serving:

Calories: 336; Total Fat: 19g; Saturated Fat: 5g; Cholesterol: 46mg; Sodium: 450mg; Total Carbs: 21g; Fiber: 4g; Protein: 22g

---

BAKED TUNA FILLETS ON CREAM OF CARROTS AND PISTACHIOS

Servings: 4

Cooking Time: 35 min

- 21 oz. tuna fillets
- 9 oz. carrots
- 2 tablespoons shelled pistachios
- 3 tablespoons extra-virgin olive oil to taste.
- One small white onion
- Salt to taste

Directions:

1. One version of the carrot cream involves cooking the vegetables in plenty of water for 10-15 minutes; in the meantime, chop the spring onion and pistachios coarsely;
2. When cooked, allow the carrots to cool and then chop them into small pieces; place them in a large blender along with the spring onion, a tablespoon of olive oil and a small amount of salt; blend until smooth and set aside;
3. Next, place the tuna fillets in a large baking dish (previously covered with a sheet of baking paper), season with a bit of salt and cover the surface with the chopped pistachios; bake at 180°C for 20 minutes;
4. When cooked, season the tuna by adding the remaining olive oil; then, arrange the fillets on a layer of carrot cream on the plate.

Per Serving:

Calories: 208, Total Fat: 10g, Saturated Fat: 2g, Cholesterol: 82mg, Sodium: 215mg, Total Carbs: 6g, Net Carbs: 3g, Fiber: 1g, Protein: 25g

CITRUS TILAPIA

Servings: 2

Cooking Time: 25 min

- Aluminum foil
- 2 tbsp garlic, minced
- 2 rosemary sprigs, stems removed, chopped
- 1 oregano sprig, stem removed, chopped
- 2 tbsp olive oil

- 2 tilapia filets, cleaned and rinsed
- 2 lemons, sliced and divided
- 2 limes, sliced and divided
- ¼ tsp fine sea salt
- ¼ tsp ground black pepper

Directions:

1. Heat the oven to 450°F, gas mark 8. Line a baking sheet with aluminum foil.
2. In a medium-sized mixing bowl, add together the minced garlic, chopped rosemary, chopped oregano, and olive oil. Mix to combine.
3. Add the tilapia fillets to the bowl, and coat generously with the olive oil mixture. Place the fillets on the prepared baking sheet.
4. Place half the lemon and lime slices on the fillets, and season with fine sea salt and ground black pepper.
5. Bake for 21 minutes, or until the fillets are cooked through, with the baking sheet in the oven. Remove from the oven.
6. Serve with your choice of side, and garnish with the remaining lemon and lime slices.

Per Serving:

Calories: 218; Total Fat: 3g; Saturated Fat: 1g; Sodium: 430mg; Total Carbs: 0g; Fiber: 0g; Protein: 45g

LEMON & LIME TUNA

Servings: 2

Cooking Time: 15 min

- 2 tsp plant-based butter
- 2 slices whole-grain bread
- 5 oz can water packed tuna, drained
- 2 tsp olive oil
- 2 tsp lite mayonnaise
- 1 tsp lemon zest
- 1 tsp lime zest

- 1 tbsp lemon juice
- 1 tbsp lime juice
- 2 tbsp red onion, finely chopped
- ½ tsp paprika (optional)
- Ground black pepper
- ¼ cup cheese blend, shredded

Directions:

1. Preheat the oven rack and position the oven rack 6 inches away from the heat source.
2. Spread plant butter thinly on both sides of the whole-grain bread slices, and place them on a baking sheet.
3. Under the broiler, toast the bread for 2 minutes on each side, or until golden brown. Make sure it doesn't burn.
4. In a glass mixing bowl, combine the drained tuna, olive oil, lite mayonnaise, lemon zest, lime zest, lemon juice, lime juice, chopped red onion, paprika (if using), and ground black pepper. Mix until fully incorporated.
5. Spread the tuna mixture between 2 slices of toasted bread and top with the shredded cheese mixture.
6. Broil for 3 mins, until the cheese has melted.

Per Serving:

Calories: 336; Total Fat: 19g; Saturated Fat: 5g; Cholesterol: 46mg; Sodium: 450mg; Total Carbs: 21g; Fiber: 4g; Protein: 22g

---

PECAN SHRIMP QUINOA

Servings: 2

Cooking Time: 15 min

- 1 tbsp avocado oil

- 1 cup brown onion, thinly sliced

- 1 cup green bell pepper, seeds removed, thinly sliced
- 2 medium Roma tomatoes, chopped
- 1 tbsp garlic, crushed
- 1½ cups reduced-sodium chicken stock
- ½ tsp paprika
- 12 oz frozen raw shrimp, thawed and peeled
- 1 cup uncooked quinoa
- ⅓ cup pecan nuts, chopped
- ⅓ cup ricotta cheese, crumbled

Directions:

1. Heat the avocado oil in a wide, heavy-bottom pan over medium-high heat. Add the sliced onion and sliced green bell pepper, and cook for 3 to 4 minutes, stirring occasionally.
2. Add the chopped tomato and crushed garlic, and cook for 1 minute until soft.
3. Add the chicken stock and paprika, and allow to boil. Add the peeled shrimp, and continue to boil.
4. Mix in the quinoa, and boil for 15 minutes, or until fully cooked. Allow to cool for 5 mins after removing the pan from the heat.
5. Top with the chopped pecan nuts and crumbled ricotta cheese, and serve.

Per Serving:

Calories: 392; Total Fat: 14g; Saturated Fat: 3g; Cholesterol: 150mg; Sodium: 490mg; Total Carbs: 40g; Fiber: 5g; Protein: 29g

WALNUT-CRUSTED HALIBUT

Servings: 2

Cooking Time: 15 min

- Aluminum foil
- 1 tbsp whole-grain mustard
- 1 tsp organic honey
- 1 tsp olive oil 1 tbsp garlic, minced
- ½ tsp ground black pepper
- 2 (4 oz) halibut fillets, skin on, scaled
- 2 tbsp unsalted walnuts, roughly chopped

Directions:

1. Heat the oven to 425°F, gas mark 7. Line a baking sheet with aluminum foil.
2. In a medium-sized mixing bowl, add together the whole-grain mustard, organic honey, olive oil, minced garlic, and ground black pepper. Mix to combine. Coat the fish fillets evenly with the mustard mixture, and place them on the baking sheet.
3. Sprinkle each fillet with 1 tbsp of chopped walnuts, and cook for 12 to 15 minutes, until the walnuts are browned, and the fish is easily flaked with a fork. Serve warm.

Per Serving:

Calories: 208, Total Fat: 10g, Saturated Fat: 2g, Cholesterol: 82mg, Sodium: 215mg, Total Carbs: 6g, Net Carbs: 3g, Fiber: 1g, Protein: 25g

---

GREEK-STYLE PAN-ROASTED SWORDFISH

Servings: 4

Cooking Time: 15 min

- 4 tbsp. extra-virgin avocado oil (divided)
- 1 small shallot, thinly sliced
- 2 tsp. crushed garlic
- 1/2 medium eggplant, diced
- 2 medium zucchinis, diced
- 1 cup whole Greek olives, pitted

- 2 cups cherry tomatoes, halved
- 4 skin-on swordfish fillets, patted dry
- Himalayan salt
- Freshly ground black pepper
- 1/4 cup green olive tapenade with harissa

Directions:

1. Set the oven to preheat to 375°F, with the wire rack in the center of the oven.
2. In a large frying pan, heat 2 tblsp of oil over medium-high heat. When the oil is nice and hot, fry the shallots and garlic for about 5 minutes, or until the shallots become translucent. Stir in the eggplant, and fry until it starts to become tender – about 3 minutes. Add the zucchini, and stir for an additional 5 minutes, until all of the vegetables are fork-tender, and crispy around the edges. Stir in the olives and tomatoes, and cook for 2 minutes, stirring constantly. Set the pan aside, off the heat.
3. Season the fish generously with salt and pepper. Heat the remaining olive oil in an oven-proof pan over medium-high heat. When the oil is hot and nice, place the fish fillets skin down in the pan, and fry for 3 minutes. The edges should just begin to become solid. Flip the fish in the pan before transferring to the oven, and baking for a final 3 minutes. The fish should be completely solid and flaky when done.
4. Top the cooked swordfish with fried vegetables and olive tapenade. Serve immediately.

Per Serving:

Calories: 605; Total Fat: 37g; Saturated Fat: 6g; Sodium: 738mg; Carbohydrates: 16g; Fiber: 6g; Protein: 54g

---

GARLIC BROILED FLOUNDER FILLETS

Servings: 4

Cooking Time: 24 min

- 1/4 tsp. Himalayan salt
- 1 tsp. freshly ground black pepper
- 1 tsp. crushed garlic
- 1 lemon, zested (segments reserved for garnish)

- 1 tbsp. avocado oil
- 4 flounder fillets, patted dry
- 1 tsp. capers, chopped
- 1/4 cup fresh parsley, chopped

Directions:

1. Using tin foil, line a large, rimmed baking pan and gently spritz with cooking spray. Set the oven broiler to preheat on low, with the wire rack about 6-inches away from the broiler.
2. Whisk together the salt, pepper, garlic, lemon zest, and avocado oil in a small glass bowl. Place the flounder fillets on the prepared baking tray, and brush with the oil mixture. Place the tray in the oven for about 10 minutes, or until the fish is no longer see-through. Broiler time may vary depending on the thickness of the fillets.
3. Plate the broiled fish, and garnish with the capers, parsley, and reserved lemon segments before serving.

Per Serving:

Calories: 151; Total Fat: 9g; Carbohydrates: 1g; Protein: 16g; Sodium: 456mg; Fiber: 0g

---

CINNAMON-GLAZED HALIBUT FILLETS

Servings: 4

Cooking Time: 20 min

- 1/4 cup extra-virgin avocado oil
- 3/4 tsp. ground cumin
- 1/2 tsp. white pepper (divided)
- 1/2 tsp. kosher salt (divided)

- 1/2 tsp. ground cinnamon
- 1 1/2 tbsp. capers, drained
- 15 oz. canned diced tomatoes, drained
- 4 halibut fillets

Directions:

1. Place the oil in a large-frying pan over medium heat. When the oil is nice and hot, add the cumin, and fry for about 1 minute, or until fragrant. Stir in 1/4 teaspoon of pepper, 1/4 teaspoon of salt, the cinnamon, capers, and canned tomatoes. Stir the sauce for about 10 minutes, or until it thickens.
2. Use paper towels to pat the fish dry. Season the fillets on both sides with the remaining salt and pepper. Nestle the seasoned fillets in the simmering sauce, and cover the pan. Allow the fish to simmer for 8-10 minutes, or until it is opaque, and flakes easily.
3. Plate the fish, and serve immediately, with the sauce ladled over the cooked fish. Enjoy!

Per Serving:

Calories: 309; Total Fat: 14g; Saturated Fat: 2g; Carbohydrates: 5g; Protein: 40g; Sodium: 525mg; Fiber: 2g

---

COCONUT-MARINATED SALMON BOWLS

Servings: 2

Cooking Time: 10 min

- 2 medium scallions, sliced
- 1 tbsp. sesame seeds
- 1/2 tsp. cayenne pepper
- 1 tsp. toasted sesame oil
- 2 tbsp. extra-virgin olive oil (plus 2 tsp.)
- 1 tbsp. coconut aminos
- 8 oz. sushi-grade wild salmon, cut into small cubes

- 1/2 medium cauliflower
- 2 tbsp. extra-virgin avocado oil
- 1 tbsp. freshly squeezed lemon juice
- Kosher salt
- White pepper
- 1 medium English cucumber, cubed
- 1 large avocado, cubed
- 1/2 nori sheet, cut into small pieces

Directions:

1. In a medium-sized bowl, whisk together the scallions, sesame seeds, cayenne pepper, toasted sesame oil, 2 tablespoons of olive oil, and coconut aminos. Add the salmon cubes, and mix to coat. Set aside on the counter while you prepare the rest of the dish.
2. Break the cauliflower into florets, and pulse on high in a blender until the chunks resemble rice. Heat the avocado oil in a large-frying pan over medium heat. When the oil is nice and hot, add the cauliflower rice, and toss for 5-7 minutes. Transfer the pan to a wooden chopping board, and toss in the lemon juice. Season to taste with salt and pepper.
3. Divide the cooked cauliflower rice between 2 bowls, and top with the marinated salmon. Garnish with the cucumber and avocado, before sprinkling with the remaining olive oil and the nori pieces. Serve immediately.

Per Serving:

Calories: 668; Total Fat: 54g; Saturated Fat: 7.8g; Carbohydrates: 20.3g; Protein: 30.9g; Fiber: 11.1g

---

TWO-WAY TILAPIA FILLETS

Servings: 6

Cooking Time: 15-20 min

- 6 tilapia fillets
- 2 cups diced tomatoes
- 1 tsp. crushed oregano
- 1 tsp. crushed sweet basil
- 2 tsp. crushed garlic flakes
- 1/2 cup roasted sweet peppers, chopped
- 1/4 cup button mushrooms, sliced

- 1/2 cup mozzarella, grated
- ½ cup Kalamata olives, pitted and diced
- 1 whole avocado, sliced
- 1/2 cup frozen corn (thawed)
- 1/2 cup feta cheese, crumbled
- 1 tsp. fresh coriander leaves, chopped

Directions:

1. Set the oven to preheat to 400F, with the wire rack in the center of the oven. Coat a large, rimmed baking tray with cooking spray.
2. Place the tilapia fillets on the prepared baking sheet, 3 per side. Divide the crushed tomatoes between the 6 fillets, using the back of a spoon to spread it out in an even layer. Top 3 of the fillets with oregano, sweet basil, crushed garlic, roasted sweet peppers, mushrooms, and mozzarella.
3. Top each of the remaining fillets with the olives, avocado, corn, feta, and fresh coriander.
4. Bake the fish in the oven for 19 minutes, or until the fish is completely opaque. Serve hot.

Per Serving:

Calories: 208; Total Fat: 4g; Saturated Fat: 2g; Carbohydrates: 5g; Protein: 34g; Sodium: 446mg; Fiber: 1g

Dessert

KIWI CAKE (NO EGGS AND NO BUTTER)

Servings: 6-7

Cooking Time: 60 min

- 6 kiwis
- 1 ½ cup wholemeal flour
- 4 tbsp stevia powder
- 4 tbsp rice oil
- 4 tbsp water
- A sachet of baking powder
- Grated lemon peel to taste

Directions:

1. Line a 10-inch cake pan with a sheet of baking paper and preheat the oven (static) to 350F;
2. Then, remove the skin from the kiwis and cut the fruit into coarse pieces;
3. In a large bowl, pour the stevia, oil, water, grated lemon peel and baking powder, then mix with a spoon; add the sifted flour gradually and continue to mix until the batter is smooth and free of lumps;
4. Add the kiwis to the mixture and mix again; then, pour the mixture into the cake tin;
5. Bake for 1 hour at 350F; let cool, portion and serve.

Per Serving:

Calories: 191; Fat: 2.3; Fiber: 1.5; Carbs: 24.4; Protein: 7.4

PEACH SORBET

Servings: 4

Preparation Time: 3 hours

- 5 Peaches, Peeled, Pitted, And Chopped
- 3/4 Cup Sugar
- Juice of 1 Lemon, or 1 Tablespoon Prepared Lemon Juice

Directions:

1. In the steel bowl of a food processor, combine all the ingredients and process until smooth.
2. Pour the mixture into a 9-by-13-inch glass pan. Cover tightly with plastic wrap. Freeze for 3 to 4 hours.
3. Remove from the freezer and scrape the sorbet into a food processor. Process until smooth. Freeze for another 30 minutes, then serve.

Per Serving:

Calories: 291; Fat: 2.3; Fiber: 1.5; Carbs: 34.4; Protein: 5.4

LIME AND WATERMELON GRANITA

Servings: 4

Preparation Time: 15 min

- 8 cups seedless watermelon chunks
- Juice of 2 limes, or 2 tablespoons prepared lime juice
- 1/2 Cup sugar
- Strips of lime zest, for garnish

Directions:

1. Combine the watermelon, lime juice, and sugar in a mixer and process until smooth. You may have to perform this in two batches.
2. After processing, stir well to combine both batches.
3. Pour the mixture into a 9-by-13-inch glass dish. Freeze for 2 to 3 hours.
4. Remove from the freezer and use a fork to scrape the top layer of ice. Leave the shaved ice on top and return to the freezer.
5. In another hour, remove from the freezer and repeat. Do this a few more times until all the ice is scraped up.
6. Serve frozen, garnished with strips of lime zest.

Per Serving:

Calories: 287; Fat: 2.a; Fiber: 1.4; Carbs: 35; Protein: 5.1

CHOCOLATE PUDDING

Servings: 4

Cooking Time: 15 min

- 1/3 cup sugar
- 1/3 cup unsweetened cocoa powder
- 3 cups unsweetened almond milk
- 1/4 Cup cornstarch
- Pinch of sea salt
- 1 teaspoon vanilla extract

Directions:

1. In a glass bowl, toss together the sugar and cocoa powder to thoroughly combine.
2. In a large-saucepan over medium heat, whisk together the cocoa mixture and 2 1/2 cups of the almond milk.
3. Bring to a boil, stirring constantly. Remove from the heat.
4. In a small bowl, whisk together the remaining 1/2 cup almond milk and cornstarch. Stir into the cocoa mixture and return to medium heat. Add the salt.
5. Stirring constantly, bring the pudding to a boil. It will begin to thicken. Boil for 1 minute. Remove the pan from the heat and add the vanilla extract. Chill before serving.

Per Serving:

Calories: 191; Fat: 2.3; Fiber: 1.5; Carbs: 24.4; Protein: 7.4

CARAMELIZED PEARS WITH BALSAMIC GLAZE

Servings: 4

Cooking Time: 15 min

- 1 cup balsamic vinegar
- 1/4 cup plus 3 tablespoons brown sugar
- 1/4 teaspoon grated nutmeg

- Pinch of sea salt
- 1/ cup coconut oil
- 4 pears, cored and cut into slices

Directions:

1. In a medium saucepan, heat the balsamic vinegar, 1/ cup of the brown sugar, the nutmeg, and salt over medium-high heat, stirring to thoroughly incorporate the sugar.
2. Allow to simmer, stirring occasionally, until the glaze reduces by half, 10 to 15 minutes.
3. Meanwhile, heat the coconut oil in a large-sauté pan over medium-high heat until it shimmers. Add the pears to the pan in a single layer.
4. Cook until they turn golden, about 5 minutes. Add the remaining 3 tablespoons brown sugar and continue to cook, stirring occasionally, until the pears caramelize, about 5 minutes more.
5. Place the pears on a plate. Drizzle with balsamic glaze and serve.

Per Serving:

Calories: 268; Fat: 2.3; Fiber: 1.5; Carbs: 25.4; Protein: 7.4

MIXED BERRIES AND CREAM

Servings: 4

Cooking Time: 10 min

- Two 15-ounce cans full-fat coconut milk
- 3 tablespoons agave
- 1/2 teaspoon vanilla extract

- 1 pint fresh blueberries
- 1 pint fresh raspberries
- 1 pint fresh strawberries, sliced

Directions:

1. Refrigerate the coconut milk overnight. The liquid will have separated from the solids when you open the can. Spoon out the solids and reserve the liquid for another purpose.
2. In a medium bowl, whisk the agave and vanilla extract into the coconut solids.
3. Divide the berries among four bowls. Top with the coconut cream. Serve immediately.

Per Serving:

Calories: 291; Fat: 2.3; Fiber: 1.5; Carbs: 25.4; Protein: 7.4

SPICED APPLE COMPOTE

Servings: 4

Cooking Time: 13 min

- 4 sweet-tart apples, cored and peeled
- 1/2 Cup apple juice
- Juice of 1 lemon
- 1/4 cup brown sugar

- 1/4 teaspoon grated nutmeg
- 1 teaspoon ground cinnamon
- Pinch of Sea Salt
- 1/2 cup chopped pecans

Directions:

1. In a saucepan, cook the apples, apple juice, lemon juice, brown sugar, nutmeg, cinnamon, Over medium-high heat, cook the apples with the sugar and salt, turning periodically, until soft, about 10 minutes.
2. Remove from the heat and set aside.
3. Meanwhile, in a dry sauté pan over medium-high heat, toast the pecans, stirring frequently, about 3 minutes.
4. Serve the compote warm topped with toasted pecans.

Per Serving:

Calories: 291; Fat: 2.3; Fiber: 1.5; Carbs: 25.4; Protein: 7.4

STRAWBERRY AND BANANA ICE CREAM

Servings: 2

Preparation Time: 5 min

- 3 cups sliced and frozen bananas
- 1 tablespoon maple syrup

- ½ teaspoon vanilla extract, unsweetened
- 1 cup strawberries, fresh

Directions:

1. Place all the ingredients in the food-processor and then pulse until smooth.
2. Divide the ice cream in two bowls and then serve.

Per Serving:

Calories: 166 Cal; Fat: 6 g; Protein: 1 g; Carbs: 30 g; Fiber: 4 g;

NO-BAKE CHOCOLATE PIE

Servings: 6

Preparation Time: 6 hours and 10 min

- 1 prepared crust of pie

For the Filling:

- 1 pound of silken tofu
- ½ teaspoon salt
- 1 teaspoon vanilla extract, unsweetened

- 2/3 cup chocolate chips, vegan, melted

- 3 tablespoons maple syrup
- 1 cup coconut milk, unsweetened

Directions:

1. Prepare the filling and for this, place all of its ingredients in a large bowl and then blend until smooth.
2. Reserve 1 cup of the filling mixture, place it in a medium bowl, add the melted chocolate and then stir until combined.
3. Place the crust in a pie pan, spoon chocolate filling it, then top with the reserved filling and make designs using a butter knife.
4. Place the pie into the refrigerator and then chill it for 4 to 6 hours in the refrigerator until firm.
5. Cut the pie into slices and then serve.

Per Serving:

Calories: 304.3 Cal; Fat: 15.4 g; Protein: 6.6 g; Carbs: 37.6 g; Fiber: 1.3 g;

RASPBERRY CRUMBLE

Servings: 2 ramekins

Preparation Time: 30 min

- 1 cup mixed berries, frozen

For the Crumble:

- ½ cup shredded coconut
- 1 teaspoon ground cinnamon
- 2 tablespoons maple syrup

- 1 teaspoon vanilla extract, unsweetened

- ½ cup macadamia nuts, chopped
- 1 teaspoon vanilla extract, unsweetened
- 3 tablespoons coconut oil

Directions:

1. Switch on the oven, then set it to 350 degrees F and let it preheat.
2. Meanwhile, place berries in a small saucepan, add vanilla extract, place the pan over medium heat, and then cook for 5 to 7 minutes until berries break down.
3. Then take two ramekins and divide berries between two ramekins.
4. Prepare the crumble and for this, take a medium bowl, add all of its ingredients in it and then stir until mixed.
5. Place the crumble-mix on top of the berries and bake for 20 to 30 minutes, or until golden brown and firm.

Per Serving:

Calories: 360.7 Cal; Fat: 1.5 g; Protein: 4.8 g; Carbs: 97.3 g; Fiber: 7 g;

CRISPY PISTACHIO BISCOTTI COOKIES

Servings: 12

Preparation Time: 1 hour

- 1 tbsp. finely grated lemon zest
- 1/4 tsp. kosher salt
- 1/2 tsp. ground nutmeg
- 1/2 tsp. ground cinnamon
- 1/2 tsp. baking soda

- 1/2 cup packed flax meal
- 2 cups almond flour
- 1 tsp. freshly squeezed lemon juice
- 1 tbsp. pure almond essence
- 2 tbsp. sunflower oil

- 1/2 tsp. pure vanilla essence
- 2 large free-range eggs
- Low-carb sweetener to taste (optional)
- 1/3 cup unsalted pistachio nuts, shells removed

Directions:

1. Set the oven to preheat to 285°F, with the wire rack in the center of the oven. Greaseproof paper should be used to line a big baking tray.
2. In a large mixing bowl, whisk together the lemon zest, salt, nutmeg, cinnamon, baking soda, flax meal, and almond flour. Use a wooden spoon to toss in the lemon juice, almond essence, sunflower oil, vanilla essence, eggs, optional sweetener, and pistachio nuts, until the dough just comes together.
3. Gather the dough into a smooth ball using your hands. Form the dough into a large log that fits the length of your prepared baking tray. Bake in the oven for about 45 minutes. Remove the log from the oven, allow it cool for 15-20 minutes on the counter before slicing into 12 equal slices with a very sharp knife.
4. Lower the oven temperature to 250°F. Lay the slices out on the same baking tray, and return the tray to the oven for a final 40 minutes. Use a spatula to gently flip the cookies halfway through the baking time.
5. Remove the tray from the oven, and let the cookies cool for an hour or two before eating.

Tip: The cookies can be stored in the cupboard in an airtight container for no more than 2 weeks.

Per Serving:

Calories: 207; Total Fat: 17.7 g; Saturated Fat: 1.9g; Carbohydrates: 7.1g; Protein: 7.2 g; Fiber: 4.2 g

---

NUTTY-TOPPED PEAR CRISP

Servings: 12

Preparation Time: 35 min

- 1/2 tsp. ground cinnamon
- 1/2 tsp. ground ginger
- 1/2 tsp. ground coriander
- 1/3 tsp. ground nutmeg
- Pinch of salt
- Pinch of freshly ground black pepper
- 1 tsp. ground arrowroot
- 1 tsp. freshly squeezed lemon juice
- 2 tbsp. cold butter, cubed
- 1/4 cup raisins
- 6 small pears, halved, cored, and sliced (1/4-inch thick slices)
- 1 tsp. chia seeds
- 1/2 cup chopped walnuts
- 1/2 cup sliced almonds

Directions:

1. Set the oven to preheat to 350F, with the wire rack in the center of the oven. Using baking spray, coat a large baking dish.
2. In a large bowl, stir together the cinnamon, ginger, coriander, nutmeg, salt, pepper, arrowroot, lemon juice, butter, raisins, and pears, until all of the ingredients are properly combined. Scrape the mixture into the baking dish that has been prepared, and spread it out evenly.
3. In a clean bowl, stir together the chia seeds, walnuts, and almonds. Strew the mixture over the top of the pears in a single layer. Place the baking dish in the oven for 35 minutes, or until the top of the crisp is golden, and the pears are crispy around the edges.
4. Let the crisp rest on the counter for 10 minutes, before serving warm with a topping of your choice, such as vanilla ice cream.

Per Serving:

Calories: 107; Total fat: 7g; Carbohydrates: 10g; Protein: 2g; Sodium: 13 mg; Fiber: 3g

21 Day Meal Plan

B. Breakfast **L.** Lunch   **D.** Dinner

DAY 1	DAY 2	DAY 3	DAY 4	DAY 5
B: Vegetable Shake **L:** Whole Wheat Linguine With Arugula Pesto **D:** Balsamic Berry Chicken	**B:** Yogurt-Topped Squash Fritters **L:** Ground Turkey Mince **D:** Shrimp Soup	**B:** Soy Yogurt And Cocoa Plumcake (No Eggs And No Butter) **L:** Spicy Crab Bites **D:** Chorizo Meat	**B:** Fruity Breakfast Couscous **L:** Two-Way Tilapia Fillets **D:** Slow Roasted Beef	**B:** Honey-Sweetened Greek Yogurt **L:** Tuna Salad **D:** Chicken Meatballs
DAY 6	**DAY 7**	**DAY 8**	**DAY 9**	**DAY 10**
B: Chocolate Pudding **L:** Walnut-Crusted Halibut **D:** Black Bean Stew	**B:** Raspberry Crumble **L:** Almond Butter Chicken **D:** Citrus Tilapia	**B:** Spinach Wraps **L:** Basil Pesto Chicken **D:** Fresh Mint & Toasted Pita Salad	**B:** Savory Mushroom Pancakes **L:** Lamb Goulash **D:** Roasted Chickpeas	**B:** Sweet Potato And Corn Chowder **L:** Cinnamon-Glazed Halibut Fillets **D:** Lime Lentil Soup
DAY 11	**DAY 12**	**DAY 13**	**DAY 14**	**DAY 15**
B: Oven-Baked Spinach Chips **L:** Couscous Salad **D:** Baked Mackerel With Artichokes And Almonds	**B:** Honey Cakes **L:** Bell Pepper Rice Soup **D:** Garlic Broiled Flounder Fillets	**B:** Zesty Fruit Parfaits **L:** Coconut-Marinated Salmon Bowls **D:** Lentil Beef Bolognese	**B:** No-Bake Chocolate Pie **L:** Greek-Style Pan-Roasted Swordfish **D:** Pork Medallions	**B:** Veggie Egg Muffins **L:** Lemon-Simmered Chicken & Artichokes **D:** Roasted Brussel Sprouts
DAY 16	**DAY 17**	**DAY 18**	**DAY 19**	**DAY 20**
B: Crispy Pistachio Biscotti Cookies **L:** Pan Fried Sirloin **D:** Broccoli Chicken Rice	**B:** Olive Turkey Patties **L:** Cabbage Turkey Soup **D:** Baked Tuna Fillets On Cream Of Carrots And Pistachios	**B:** Blueberry Waffles **L:** Delightful Stuffed Lamb With Peppers **D:** Whole Wheat Barley With Herbs	**B:** Strawberry And Banana Ice Cream **L:** Parmesan Pork Chops **D:** Vietnamese Beef Soup	**B:** Mediterranean Egg Scramble **L:** Zesty Vinaigrette Potato Salad **D:** Pecan Shrimp Quinoa
DAY 21				
B: Spiced Apple Compote **L:** Cheesy Salmon & Vegetable Soup **D:** Garlic Turkey Skewers				

Culinary Reference Table

Unit:	Equals:	Also equals:
1 teaspoon	1/3 tablespoon	1/6 fluid ounce
1 tablespoon	3 teaspoons	1/2 fluid ounce
1/8 cup	2 tablespoons	1 fluid ounce
1/4 cup	4 tablespoons	2 fluid ounces
1/3 cup	1/4 cup plus 4 teaspoons	2 3/4 fluid ounces
1/2 cup	8 tablespoons	4 fluid ounces
1 cup	1/2 pint	8 fluid ounces
1 pint	2 cups	16 fluid ounces
1 quart	4 cups	32 fluid ounces
1 liter	1 quart plus 1/4 cup	4 1/4 cups
1 gallon	4 quarts	16 cups

Printed in Great Britain
by Amazon